D1516777

WITHDRAWN

BODY LANGUAGE AT WORK

MARY HARTLEY, the author of *The Good Stress Guide* and *Managing Anger at Work*, was born in London and lives in Guildford. She divides her time between writing books and articles, and leading courses and workshops in aspects of personal development.

Overcoming Common Problems Series

A full list of titles is available from Sheldon Press,
1 Marylebone Road, London NW1 4DU, and on our website at
www.sheldonpress.co.uk

Overcoming Common Problems Series

Overcoming Common Problems Series

Overcoming Common Problems

BODY LANGUAGE AT WORK

Mary Hartley

sheldon **PRESS**

First published in Great Britain in 2003 by
Sheldon Press
1 Marylebone Road
London NW1 4DU

Illustrations created by Hardlines Ltd, Park Street, Charlbury, Oxford.

British Library Cataloguing-in-Publication Data

A catalogue record for this book is available from the British Library

ISBN 0–85969–877–7

1 3 5 7 9 10 8 6 4 2

Typeset by Deltatype Limited, Birkenhead, Merseyside
Printed in Great Britain by Mackays of Chatham

Contents

1

What is Body Language?

We all communicate with one another through a variety of means. We express our thoughts and feelings through words, spoken and written. At work, words are the currency of communication. Conversations, instructions, agreements, contracts, discussions, gossip, interviews and meetings all depend on verbal language, whether we are communicating face to face or on the phone, through e-mails, letters, memos, scribbled notes or formal documents. In our dealings with other people, as we send and receive messages and information we use words to make our meaning clear.

However, another powerful means of communication takes place without a word being spoken. We send messages about ourselves and draw conclusions about other people through our appearance, our facial expressions, how we stand and move, how we sit, how we gesture with our hands and arms. When we speak, the sound of our voice – its tone, pace, stress and intonation – affects what we say and can change the meaning of the words that we utter. We even communi-

cate in the way that we use silence. Body language refers to the non-verbal signals we send and receive, intentionally or unintentionally. Every aspect of our face-to-face communication with other people is influenced by body language. As well as communicating without words, our non-verbal signals can back up what we say and reinforce it. Our body language can also contradict our words, sometimes without our realizing that this is happening.

Like any language, body language has rules and systems that to some extent are learned through imitation, and to some extent are determined by our culture. A number of body signals – for example, smiling to express pleasure and frowning to show displeasure – seem to be universally understood. Other non-verbal signs, such as hand and finger gestures indicating approval or abuse, have different meanings in different cultures. If you misinterpret signals, or if other people misinterpret the signals that you send, you are likely to end up in a situation in which, at the very least, communication is ineffective, and which at its worst could be extremely embarrassing and destructive to working relationships. On the other hand, when body language is effective – that is to say, when verbal and non-verbal messages are in harmony and reinforce one another, and are mutually recognized and understood – communication is clear and powerful and satisfactory outcomes are much more easily attained.

Scientists, psychologists, sociologists and other observers of human behaviour have been formulating theories about body language for over one hundred years. Desmond Morris caught the public's attention with books such as *Manwatching* (1977), which explores the similarities between animals and human beings as well as the universality of gestures. Morris's work focuses on the area of study pioneered by Charles Darwin, whose book *The Expression of Emotion in Man and Animals* (1872) draws attention to some of the universal aspects of the way we communicate through facial expression and gestures.

Research conducted by the psychologist Albert Mehrabian (*Silent Messages*, 1971) explores the power of non-verbal communication. Mehrabian's observations of the effectiveness of verbal presentations, when applied to everyday face-to-face encounters, suggest that the actual words spoken have the least impact. The words themselves account for only 7 per cent of the communication. That means that 93 per cent is non-verbal. Of this percentage, 38 per cent of the impact is created by what your voice sounds like – its tone and pitch, how you pace

your speech, how loudly you speak, your accent. The remaining 55 per cent is the visual impression conveyed by aspects such as your facial expressions and body movement. Most of our communication is non-verbal, and yet although we think carefully about what we are going to say, we often do not give careful consideration to what we convey through the way we speak and how we move.

Psychologist Michael Argyle (*The Psychology of Interpersonal Behaviour*, 1973) observes that we exchange information about facts and events through words, but that we form and maintain personal relationships through non-verbal communication. The ability to control and manage your body language and to respond sensitively to others' non-verbal messages will add to your effectiveness at work and enhance the quality of your communication.

Scene 1: Gareth's interview

Gareth is about to be interviewed for the position of warehouse manager. He takes deep breaths to steady his nerves, and mentally rehearses the answers that he has prepared. Gareth knows that he is less experienced than the other applicants, but he has established good relationships with his co-workers and feels that he would do the job well.

Gareth tries to hide his nerves. He leans back in his chair with his legs spread in what he hopes is a confident pose and, to stop his hands shaking, he joins his fingertips together so that they form the shape of a church steeple.

When Gareth leaves the room, one of the two interviewers says, 'He looked really arrogant, as if he thinks he is superior. I can't see him getting on well with the warehouse team.'

Figure 1 *Seeming over-confident*

Gareth does not realize that the steeple gesture he is using can indicate over-confidence and self-importance. This impression is reinforced by the way that he sits (Figure 1). Gareth's body language gives a misleading impression, and the interviewer is influenced more by Gareth's non-verbal signals than by what he says in the interview. In general, when there is conflict between the words that we use and the body signals that we send, our body language will override what we say. So although Gareth gave examples and anecdotes to illustrate his approachability and his ability to maintain good relationships, his posture and the way he positioned his hands gave the opposite impression. Gareth will have greater success at his next interview if he learns how to manage his body language to give a more accurate representation of himself.

Of course, the interviewer also needs to learn not to read body signals in isolation. (You will find out more about this as you read on.)

Scene 2: Sonia is about to lose a customer

Sonia sits in the car park, thinking about the meeting she has just had with one of her company's major buyers. Although Lucy said that she liked the new designs and would be putting in another order, Sonia feels uneasy. There was something that did not quite ring true. She mentally visualizes the meeting, and recalls the way that Lucy sat with her legs and her arms crossed, and the way she kept glancing away as she spoke (Figure 2).

On an impulse, Sonia phones Lucy's assistant. 'I just feel that, in spite of what she said, Lucy is not going to order from us.'

'To tell you the truth,' says Lucy's assistant, 'she has found a cheaper supplier, and is thinking of going with them. She didn't want to tell you because she likes you, and she's been so pleased with your company's products and service.'

'Thanks,' says Sonia. Now that she knows Lucy's reservations, she can discuss the matter further.

Figure 2 *Looking unreceptive*

Sonia's accurate interpretation of Lucy's body language means that she is able to take immediate action to try to keep her custom. In this case, Sonia's response to non-verbal signals has a positive effect.

Body Language and Your Image

Your image at work is the way that you appear to others. Even if you feel that you do not have a particular image, other people will have formed an impression of you and your personality – and this applies both to those with whom you work closely and to those with whom you may never have exchanged a word. The fact is that it is impossible not to communicate ideas about yourself. Just as you form impressions of other people, so they are taking in the signals that you give through your appearance, the way you walk and talk, your gestures. Difficulties and misunderstandings arise when you are unaware of the impression you create, or when you think that you come across in a certain way, whereas in fact you are perceived quite differently.

As you will have gathered from the previous comments, much of the impression that you make on other people is created through your non-verbal behaviour. Your knowledge of the non-verbal signals that you send and receive can help you to manage the impression you make at work. You can control your behaviour so that you give the messages that you want to give, and as far as possible make your outward appearance match your inner intentions. Although body language is not an exact science, and is always open to different interpretations, you can minimize the possibility of giving a false impression of yourself.

You can also behave and present yourself in a way that will help you to achieve your personal work objectives. People will see the image that you project. If you appear to be, for example, efficient and well organized, others will respond to you accordingly. If you create

ACTIVITY 1: Tuning in to body language

(a) Video-record about 15 minutes of a television drama or soap opera that is not familiar to you. Watch the segment with the sound turned off. How much of the action can you understand? What feelings and emotions do you identify? Jot down your findings in the chart below:

Scene	What's going on	What feelings are shown
1		
2		
3		
4		

Now watch the extract with the sound on. How accurate were your assumptions?_____

(b) Try the exercise the other way round. Video-record 15 minutes of a similar programme, and watch it with your back turned so that you can hear but not see. Then watch the segment with sound as well as vision. How do the characters' actions and facial expressions add to your interpretation of what is happening?

_____

_____

_____

an impression of being friendly and approachable, others will react to these qualities. Managing the impression that you make on other people will help you in all kinds of work situations, such as appraisal and selection interviews, dealing with customers, clients, students, pupils and patients, interpersonal relationships with your team and your manager, giving presentations, handling negotiations – in fact, the whole range of work experiences.

ACTIVITY 2: Your work image

What personal and professional qualities and attitudes do you want to communicate through your appearance, your behaviour and your body language? For each of the following descriptions, circle the number that shows how important the quality is to you:

	Not important						Very important		
Competent	1	2	3	4	5	6	7	8	9
Approachable	1	2	3	4	5	6	7	8	9
Confident	1	2	3	4	5	6	7	8	9
Decisive	1	2	3	4	5	6	7	8	9
Serious	1	2	3	4	5	6	7	8	9
Good fun	1	2	3	4	5	6	7	8	9
Powerful	1	2	3	4	5	6	7	8	9
Reliable	1	2	3	4	5	6	7	8	9
Friendly	1	2	3	4	5	6	7	8	9
Influential	1	2	3	4	5	6	7	8	9
Persuasive	1	2	3	4	5	6	7	8	9
Ambitious	1	2	3	4	5	6	7	8	9
Conscientious	1	2	3	4	5	6	7	8	9
Organized	1	2	3	4	5	6	7	8	9
Creative	1	2	3	4	5	6	7	8	9
Sympathetic	1	2	3	4	5	6	7	8	9

WHAT IS BODY LANGUAGE?

Honest	1	2	3	4	5	6	7	8	9
Authoritative	1	2	3	4	5	6	7	8	9
Risk-taking	1	2	3	4	5	6	7	8	9
Rule-breaking	1	2	3	4	5	6	7	8	9
Rule-keeping	1	2	3	4	5	6	7	8	9
Goal-orientated	1	2	3	4	5	6	7	8	9
Problem-solving	1	2	3	4	5	6	7	8	9
Systematic	1	2	3	4	5	6	7	8	9
In touch with feelings	1	2	3	4	5	6	7	8	9
Competitive	1	2	3	4	5	6	7	8	9
Prudent	1	2	3	4	5	6	7	8	9
Task-orientated	1	2	3	4	5	6	7	8	9
People-orientated	1	2	3	4	5	6	7	8	9

Add your own ideas:

(a) _____	1	2	3	4	5	6	7	8	9
(b) _____	1	2	3	4	5	6	7	8	9
(c) _____	1	2	3	4	5	6	7	8	9
(d) _____	1	2	3	4	5	6	7	8	9

Your Work Values and Goals

The qualities and attributes that you have identified in Activity 2 as central to your image at work not only reflect the way that you want to be seen, but also give some indication of what is important in your working life. Once you have a clear idea of what you want to accomplish you can manage your behaviour, and the signals you give, in order to reflect your goals and values.

ACTIVITY 3: Goals and values

Which three aspects of work are most important to you? You could choose from the following list, and add your own ideas:

Making money	Working in a team	Being a leader
Making a difference	Being challenged	Enjoying what I do
Dealing with the public	Companionship	Having power
Working independently	Being praised by customers/clients	Sense of accomplishment
Self-actualization	Having responsibility	Being creative

1 _____

2 _____

3 _____

Once you have identified what is important to you, choose one or more work goals. Think about areas in which your behaviour and the impression you give to others will contribute towards your success. A couple of examples are given for you below:

Important to me	Work goal
e.g. Being a leader	To be promoted to manager
e.g. Dealing with the public	To respond pleasantly to difficult customers

(a) _____

(b) _____

(c) _____

What Body Language Will Do For You

Developing the skills of body language will enhance every aspect of your communication at work, and help you to accomplish what matters to you. You can modify and control your behaviour, and influence the way that others see you and respond to you, without sacrificing your own personality or pretending to be something you are not. Of course, there are times when we need to mask our true feelings, but this does not mean that we are being false or deceitful.

In all situations, we have a range of behaviours from which we choose the most appropriate. We rarely behave in a totally natural and instinctive way; all of us have adapted our natural instincts to meet the needs of society, and our behaviour reflects attitudes and skills that we have learnt and developed. For example, you may well feel nervous as you stand up to give a presentation, but you will wish to appear confident, and a confident manner is not only appropriate to the success of your delivery, but essential. If there were an industrial accident in the area that you supervise, you would probably wish to appear calm and in control of procedures, no matter how panicky you felt inside. In both these cases, your intention is to give an impression that fits the situation, and reflects how you wish to handle it. In the example given in the previous exercise, those who wish to be promoted to manager will stand a better chance of achieving this goal if their body language is seen to be consistent with the qualities and attitudes that the particular company requires for such a position. You can acquire the ability to manage your self-presentation so that the messages that you give match your intention, and your communication displays confidence and integrity.

What Body Language Will Not Do For You

Do not assume that knowing about body language is a sure-fire route to fooling others about your real personality, abilities and intentions, or that you will be able to read other people's minds and identify their real personalities, abilities and intentions from the non-verbal signals you pick up.

Although non-verbal behaviour can be learnt and controlled, this does not guarantee that you will be able to hide any discrepancies between your real feelings and the impression you want to create. Our communicative behaviour is subject to *leakage*. This term refers to the unconscious signals we give that leak out information about our real feelings and attitudes. Small physical gestures of which you are unaware can reveal emotional states such as anger, tension or nervousness. Tapping your fingers or feet, rapid blinking, fiddling with a tie or with jewellery may communicate messages that contradict your words and your other non-verbal signals. These microgestures are tiny and over in a flash, but if they are picked up they can provide an insight into what is going on behind the surface impression. When we speak of having a sixth sense or a hunch about a person, quite often the fact is that we have subconsciously recognized and responded to such signals.

9

When our outward gestures match our words and our intentions, we display *congruence*. This means that everything fits together, and there are no significant contradictory or incongruent elements in our communication. For example, you may have experienced the person who smiles in greeting and shakes your hand warmly, but whose eyes are searching the room for someone else (presumably someone more interesting or important!) to speak to. Of the contradictory messages conveyed by this person's body language, it is likely that the recipient will respond most strongly to the message that suggests lack of real interest.

Body language signals cannot be read in isolation. If you try to apply a straight rule of thumb, assuming that a particular gesture, facial expression or posture always has a particular meaning, you are likely to misinterpret people's behaviour. Our non-verbal signals do not exist in isolation, but in *clusters*. To be understood, each signal needs to be seen in relation to the signals that surround it, just as spoken or written words acquire their meaning from the whole sentence in which they appear. Body language signals should be seen in combination with one another, and in the context of the whole communication event and the situation in which it occurs. After all, you would not understand someone's meaning if you heard only one or two words of a spoken sentence. Also, it is possible that some actions are purely physical responses without any psychological significance. For example, shifting position in a seat may just be an attempt to get more comfortable, blinking rapidly might be a way of removing a stray eyelash. Do not place too much emphasis on individual actions without considering the situation as a whole and the person's communicative behaviour as a whole.

Finally, do not underestimate or ignore the power of words. As you know, words by themselves do not constitute the message, but, in most situations in the workplace, what is said is important. Body language accompanies and complements speech. Do not rush to make judgements based solely on non-verbal messages, and do not try to make your personal impact entirely through body language. All non-verbal signals are part of the complex process of communication, and should be seen in relation to other behaviours and the contexts in which they occur.

Achieving Congruence

The closer the match between your inner state and your behaviour, the more convincing your body language signals will be. Having a positive self-image is central to managing the impression that you have of yourself and that you convey to others. If you see yourself in a negative light, your body language will convey lack of confidence and self-esteem. A vicious circle is then set up as others respond to your low self-value – and thereby, as you see it, confirming your lack of self-worth.

A way of breaking this cycle and managing a positive impression of yourself is to act yourself into a particular state of mind. Your mind will actually follow your body. For example, if you

ACTIVITY 4: The importance of context

(a) Certain non-verbal actions are often interpreted as having particular meanings. Folded arms are thought to create a barrier; yawning is thought to indicate boredom; head scratching is sometimes interpreted as a sign of stress. What meanings might these gestures have in the following situations?

	Folded arms	Yawning	Head scratching
With a friend			
In a meeting			
In a selection interview			
Being reprimanded			
With a customer			
Chatting to a co-worker			

(b) What message is conveyed when someone frowns? Think of six possibilities:

1

2

3

4

5

6

ACTIVITY 5: Acting the part

Choose someone at work whose body language displays qualities that *you* would like to show. It could be someone who appears confident, or whose non-verbal signals suggest is a good listener. Focus on some aspects of their behaviour (such as their gestures, or the way they walk and sit, or their tone of voice) and practise behaving in a similar way. Identify occasions when you will use that type of body language. Use the chart below to help you keep on track:

Aspect of behaviour	*When I will use it*	*Comments on result*
1		
2		
3		
4		
5		
6		

want to feel lively and energetic, think about how your body behaves when you are feeling this way. Remember how you stand and walk, your facial expression, how you move your head. Once you have mentally tuned into your body's pattern, take it on physically. Follow your body's natural pattern, behave as you usually do when you are in an energetic frame of mind, and you will access that energized feeling. (Incidentally, this is a great way to use the language of your body to get yourself out of a slump at work.) So, if you want to be seen as authoritative, learn and use the body language that conveys authority. Others will then respond to your impression of authority, and this strengthens your self-confidence. You will begin to feel more authoritative. The way that you behave influences the way that you feel and the way that other people behave towards you, which in turn affects the way that you feel about yourself. The vicious circle can become a circle of confidence.

2

First Impressions

Appearances say a lot. Before we have any verbal interaction with people, we make an immediate judgement about certain things – such as their gender and age range. We also take in information about someone's racial and cultural background.

Our judgements are based on the cues we pick up from elements of people's physical appearance as well as from the way they dress and behave. Physical aspects such as the size and shape of our bodies tend to be more permanent and less easily changed than our style of dress and the image we portray.

It has been suggested that there is some connection between aspects of our inner selves and our physical characteristics. For example, a habitually tense posture might have developed as a result of someone's nervous or worried outlook on life, or someone who has experienced a lot of physical pain might reflect this in facial lines that have developed through tension or frowning.

Standing Tall

Your posture and the way that you stand and walk give some idea of your personality and state of mind. In conversation and interaction with others, your posture will change as you respond and adjust to different people and situations, but you probably have a distinctive, habitual way of standing and walking. You might slouch, or hunch your shoulders, or keep your head bent down – all positions that could be seen as depicting a lack of confidence. An upright, balanced posture sends a positive message. People who stand and move with their head raised, and their shoulders square and even, communicate a sense of self-esteem and confidence. They also look and feel more energetic than those whose posture suggests uncertainty.

In Figure 3, the figure on the right has an upright head, square shoulders and straight, relaxed arms and legs. The impression created by the posture is one of confidence and calm self-

Use a mirror to help you with this. Keep your head up, evenly balanced and in alignment with your spine. Do not push your jaw forward, or pull your chin in. Imagine that an invisible string is suspending your head from the ceiling. Check that your shoulders are evenly balanced, not hunched or rounded, and that your torso and hips are facing straight ahead, not twisted to one side. Keep your weight equally balanced on both feet. When you are satisfied with the posture that you have achieved, practise it as much as you can. It takes a long time to undo years of bad posture habits, but by reminding yourself every now and again throughout the day to stand straight and stretch your spine, you will begin to make beneficial changes.

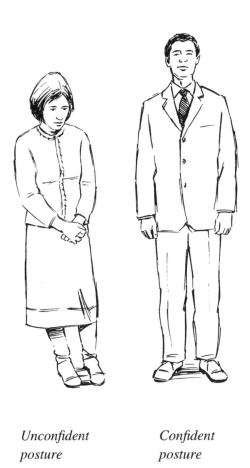

Unconfident posture   *Confident posture*

Figure 3

Facial Expression

What is your facial expression when it is in repose – that is, when you are not interacting with someone or responding to a situation? Your habitual expression might be a slight frown, or a turned-down mouth. People will assume that you have personal characteristics associated with the facial expression. Without being aware of it, you might come across as grumpy or worried, or aloof and haughty. Your facial expression is one of the first things that people notice about you, and there is general agreement about the personal qualities communicated by particular expressions.

assurance. The figure on the left is stooping slightly, with head down and one leg bent, creating an impression of lack of confidence.

15

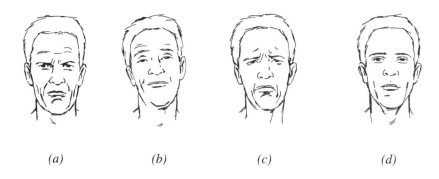

(a)   *(b)*   *(c)*   *(d)*

Figure 4 *Facial expressions*

ACTIVITY 7: Identifying facial expressions
Which of the facial expressions in Figure 4 shows:

1 Happiness _____

2 Sadness _____

3 Anger _____

4 Interest _____

Answers: 1(b); 2(c); 3(a); 4(d).

The power of a smile

We respond positively to a smile. If you smile when you greet people you indicate a willingness to be pleasant and to communicate, and your smile is likely to be returned.

False smiles are revealed through other body signals. When we give a genuine smile our eyes wrinkle a little at the edges and our mouth curves spontaneously. Non-genuine smiles do not reach the eyes, and the mouth can look fixed or twisted.

ACTIVITY 8: Your public face
Imagine that you have just caught sight of someone who you are pleased to see. What expression does your face assume? It is probably relaxed, open and friendly, with your eyes a little wide and your mouth turning up slightly. You could try to make this your normal facial expression. Practise getting it right. You might have to use your facial muscles to unfurrow your brow, to lift your eyebrows, and to stop your mouth from turning down. The exercise involved in this should improve your facial tone as well as helping you to present a positive face to the world!

16

ACTIVITY 9: Attitudes to work dress

Check out your own perceptions about dress and work performance. Put a tick in the appropriate box:

	Strongly agree	Agree	Disagree	Strongly disagree
1 I judge the standard of service I am likely to receive from the overall dress and appearance of staff.	☐	☐	☐	☐
2 It doesn't matter how you are dressed, it's how you do the job that matters.	☐	☐	☐	☐
3 Being dressed appropriately makes you feel confident.	☐	☐	☐	☐
4 People who don't dress smartly are less likely to be promoted.	☐	☐	☐	☐
5 Comfort is more important than appearance.	☐	☐	☐	☐
6 I could not respect a manager who did not dress suitably.	☐	☐	☐	☐
7 How I am dressed affects the way that I feel.	☐	☐	☐	☐
8 How I am dressed affects the way that I behave.	☐	☐	☐	☐

Add your own ideas:

	Strongly agree	Agree	Disagree	Strongly disagree
9 _____	☐	☐	☐	☐
10 _____	☐	☐	☐	☐
11 _____	☐	☐	☐	☐
12 _____	☐	☐	☐	☐

The Language of Clothes

The way you dress makes a statement about you. Whatever your reasons for wearing particular clothes, other people will interpret your appearance and draw conclusions about a range of aspects of you, from what kind of job you do to what kind of personality you have. Similarly, your initial judgement of others is based on the way that they are dressed. Dress has its own language and codes, in which certain meanings are attached to particular items, and certain types of dress are considered appropriate for particular circumstances. If your style of attire is remarkably different from what is expected, people will probably wonder why you have made your particular choices and, depending on the context, might feel ill at ease, threatened in some way, or just plain annoyed.

We all have inbuilt ideas, conscious or unconscious, about what constitutes appropriate dress for work. Often we only realize that we have these expectations when they are not met or are challenged in some way. We also link people's appearance with their ability, and tend to have confidence in those whose dress seems to reflect an appropriate professionalism.

Uniform style

Official uniform

Work uniforms have the function of indicating the job that someone does. Police and security forces, the armed forces, workers in the medical sector, retail and service staff are just some examples of types of work in which a uniform communicates people's role – and, sometimes, their status as well. Wearing a uniform affects the behaviour of those who wear it and those with whom they interact. The act of putting on a uniform signifies that you belong to a certain group, and certain types of behaviour will be expected of you.

Although uniforms are occasionally redesigned to create a more contemporary look, it is a characteristic of a uniform that it meets the purposes of identification, not of fashion. As well as the actual clothes, there are often requirements about the kind of hairstyle, shoes and jewellery that are thought to be appropriate. If you try to customize your uniform, whether it is to feel more comfortable or to make a personal style statement, you send conflicting messages and may well undermine confidence in your work performance.

Scene 3: The car hire firm

Hanif runs a car hire and taxi business. He gets a lot of work from airport customers, and has built up a list of regular clients. His drivers wear a uniform consisting of a smart jacket and trousers with a white shirt and black shoes. Hanif thinks that one of the reasons for the company's success is the professional appearance of the drivers.

Hanif hears that one of the companies who use him regularly has gone to a rival firm, and he phones to find out why. His contact sounds quite embarrassed.

ACTIVITY 10: Uniform qualities

What qualities do you associate with the following items and characteristics of uniform? Match up the qualities from the list and the item of uniform described. You can use the same qualities more than once:

Item of uniform   *Qualities*

Peaked cap _____

Overalls _____

Blouse and skirt _____

Company sweatshirt _____

Hat _____

Tailored jacket _____

Apron _____

Braided jacket _____

High-heeled shoes _____

Colour of uniform   *Qualities*

Red _____

Black _____

Blue and white _____

List of qualities

Efficient	Traditional	Managerial	Approachable
Authoritative	Approachable	Forward-looking	Scientific
Fun	Clinical	Casual	Caring
Reliable	Hands-on	Practical	

'No, you never let us down, and no, you are not too expensive. We just felt that maybe your drivers aren't of quite the same standard as they used to be.'

When Hanif talks to his drivers, he notices the appearance of the two recent additions to his team. Although they are wearing the basic uniform, one of them has on a T-shirt instead of a shirt and is wearing trainer-type shoes, while the other has several rings in one ear and multi-coloured dyed hair.

Hanif has to ensure that the appearance of his drivers reflects the company's established image, or he may lose more customers.

Unofficial uniform
Some places of work do not have a uniform, but have dress codes that make certain requirements. These are usually unwritten, and you pick them up from observation. The accepted forms of dress will vary within each individual workplace.

ACTIVITY 11: Your workplace dress code

What is the unofficial dress code at your own place of work? Tick the televant boxes. (If it is more appropriate, choose a workplace with which you are familiar.)

	Definitely	Not at all
Do people dress informally?	☐	☐
Do people dress fashionably?	☐	☐
Do people dress expensively?	☐	☐
Are business suits expected?	☐	☐
Do people often wear new outfits?	☐	☐
Are the same kinds of shoes worn?	☐	☐
Do people wear the same kind of jewellery?	☐	☐
Is there a range of hair colours and styles?	☐	☐
Do people use the same kind of bag or case?	☐	☐

You might find that certain sections or departments have their own code, perhaps according to the nature of the work, or the age of the people concerned. Of course you can choose not to follow the dress code, but, if you make this decision, you may be perceived as lacking commitment, and your work performance may be viewed in a negative light.

Matching the environment

For some areas of work, there are generally shared ideas about dress, although even within particular sections of the profession there may be variations.

ACTIVITY 12: Which one is the lawyer?

(a) Paul wears a dark business suit, polished shoes, and carries his papers in a leather briefcase.

(b) Stephen wears jeans and a leather jacket, and carries his papers in a backpack.

Answer: _____

Look at Activity 12. In fact, they are both lawyers. Paul works in a large city firm, and Stephen works in an inner-city legal aid centre. Each dresses in a way that is appropriate for the context. If Paul wore Stephen's kind of clothes to work, he would appear very bizarre and would not inspire confidence. If Stephen dressed as Paul

does, he might well give the impression of being an unapproachable, establishment figure.

On the other hand, you could argue that Stephen needs to impress his clients with his professional ability as much as Paul does, and that formal clothes would help to create confidence in him. We feel secure when people's dress is suitable for the job they do and the environment in which they work. It is probably true to say that in these cases we do not even notice what they are wearing. When we feel that the understood dress code has been transgressed, however, we may experience serious discomfort, and withdraw our custom or our co-operation.

Scene 4: Rita's interview clothes

Rita works in a large financial firm, and often has to meet clients. For work she wears well-cut, conservative dark suits and unobtrusive jewellery, and keeps her hair short and well-groomed. She carries a black leather briefcase, and wears good-quality shoes. Rita's office dress is similar to that worn by the other women at work, and her smart and professional image creates confidence in her abilities and in the services that her company offers.

Rita applies for a managerial role in a public relations company, and wears her usual kind of clothes for the interview. However, in the context of the different workplace her dress appears to be dull and dowdy. In this second environment, the women dress to make more of an impact with clients, and to reflect an upbeat, contemporary approach.

Dress for success

It is possible to interpret the idea of successful dressing in two ways. The first focuses on whether the clothes and appearance are suitable for the particular job, and whether they enable the wearer of them to perform well. If that is the case, then you are dressed for success.

Often the concept of successful dressing is linked with advancement and promotion. If one of your work goals is to be promoted, then the way that you dress could help or hinder you in achieving what you want to achieve.

ACTIVITY 13: What is suitable?

How would you feel about the following examples of people's work wear and appearance? Tick the relevant box:

	Comfortable	Quite comfortable	Uncomfortable
(a) A dentist in bikers' leathers.	☐	☐	☐
(b) A fashion boutique assistant with several facial piercings.	☐	☐	☐
(c) A teacher with several facial piercings.	☐	☐	☐
(d) Air cabin crew in jeans.	☐	☐	☐
(e) A hospital receptionist with a tattoo.	☐	☐	☐

Individual touches

The advice that is often given is to dress for the job that you want, not the job that you currently have. Use your judgement as to how far this practice will help you to climb the work ladder, and its possible effect on your co-workers. Also, use your judgement about other ways in which any attempt to stand out from the crowd will be perceived. You might feel that your cartoon character tie shows that you have a fun personality, but others may not see it in the same way, and it might just have a negative effect on your promotion prospects. Or, you might know that your droopy cardigan is at the cutting edge of current fashion, but unless you work in an environment where this will be recognized, a more effective choice might be a jacket or similar garment that is less fashionable, but that is more immediately associated with responsibility and authority.

'Dress-down days'

Some companies tried an interesting experiment in the 1990s when they designated one day a week, usually Friday, when employees were encouraged to leave their business wear at home

---

ACTIVITY 14: Moving up

What is the dress code for senior people in your workplace? Choose two people who hold the kind of position to which you aspire. Make some notes under the following headings:

	Dress	Accessories	Hairstyle
Person a			
Person b			

---

and go to work dressed in casual clothes. Other companies extended the policy to cover the whole week. One of the objectives of the experiment was to break down barriers between different levels of worker and to generate more communication and teamwork. It was also thought that dressing casually would make people feel more comfortable and increase productivity. The movement to more casual attire was started by computer companies in the United States and seemed to reflect the egalitarian culture of the dotcom industry.

However, the scheme has had mixed success.

Some companies in the United Kingdom have abandoned the practice in favour of a return to a policy of formal business dress. One American investment bank has now asked men to wear a suit and tie, and women to wear suits, trouser suits or dresses. Both employees and employers found it difficult to manage the scheme of 'dress-down days'. Workers had difficulty gauging what kind of casual dress would be appropriate, and found the experience impractical and expensive, while employers found that dressing casually encouraged lateness and absenteeism.

The Language of Objects

Your choice of personal items adds to the impression you create. The type of cellphone you have and what ringing tone you choose, the kind of diary and pen you use, how you embellish and personalize your workspace, and the items that you have in your car will all evoke responses from others.

Scene 5: Personal objects

Patricia has a photograph of her two children on her desk, while Marti has a photograph of herself scuba diving. Patricia is perceived as being kind and sympathetic, and people confide in her. Marti is thought of as being confident and dynamic, and people tend to discuss work matters with her. Kali carries a

---

ACTIVITY 15: Whose mug?

Look at the following description of the coffee mugs lined up on a shelf in the kitchen area at work. What impression do you receive of the personality of the owner of each mug? Decide how positive or negative a response you have, and circle the appropriate number:

Description of mug	Personality	Positive								Negative
(a) Has a picture of cute kittens.		1	2	3	4	5	6	7	8	9
(b) Has a picture of a National Trust property.		1	2	3	4	5	6	7	8	9
(c) A holiday souvenir.		1	2	3	4	5	6	7	8	9
(d) Has a football team's badge.		1	2	3	4	5	6	7	8	9
(e) Chipped and dirty.		1	2	3	4	5	6	7	8	9
(f) Has an art gallery's logo.		1	2	3	4	5	6	7	8	9
(g) Has a funny slogan.		1	2	3	4	5	6	7	8	9
(h) A bone china cup and saucer.		1	2	3	4	5	6	7	8	9

---

briefcase to work, while Tom uses a carrier bag. Kali's briefcase could contain her lunch, a magazine and a sweater that she wants to return to the store in her lunch hour. In Tom's carrier bag there could be some urgent work that he had taken home to finish. The contents could be reversed. The point is that Kali's choice of receptacle gives a more professional air.

The Language of Places

Objects such as rooms, furniture, stationery, types of work equipment and so on send messages about companies and organizations. The way that a company presents itself indicates something about its ethos and its attitude to employees and clients.

Your first impression of an organization may be its advertising and literature. Choices that are made about the kind of typeface, colours, images and icons used on items such as brochures, letterheads, flyers and websites reveal where the organization places itself in the market and how it sees itself.

A reception area with a warm and welcoming atmosphere indicates a people-orientated approach, perhaps suitable for a services industry, whereas a more austere presentation could indicate that the product is the most important thing. A smart public area and shabby staff facilities suggest that the company is more concerned with its public image than with the people who work there.

Scene 6: Public areas

Pamela goes into her local travel agency to book a holiday. There is a half-eaten sandwich on the counter and unpacked boxes of brochures are on the floor. The posters on display are a little tatty and tired-looking. She goes up to the counter and has to wait for a few minutes for the assistant to finish a phone call and notice that she is waiting for attention.

Pamela has a negative first response to a company that seems to pay little attention to the impression that customers receive. She receives an impression of sloppiness and lack of attention to detail.

Bob and Thea are choosing a school for their son. As they enter the reception area they notice the wall displays of children's work and the photographs of classes involved in different activities. The person at the desk is speaking on the phone and at the same time handing a sticking plaster to one of the three children waiting for attention. She smiles at them as they approach. There is a half-drunk cup of coffee in front of her.

Bob and Thea have a positive first impression of a busy, child-orientated school. They respond to the signs of friendliness and subconsciously pick up signals that although staff are busy, the children's needs are not neglected.

ACTIVITY 16: Messages from your workplace

What impression is created by your place of work?

Buildings _____

Decor _____

Furniture _____

Arrangement of rooms _____

3

Face to Face

Hello and Goodbye

We convey particular messages in the manner that we greet people and the way that we finish the encounter. Managing the initial greeting can be tricky if you are uncertain about how to deal with matters such as shaking hands and taking seats. Generally it is the person in the more dominant role who initiates the handshake and indicates the seating arrangements. If you are welcoming someone, hold out your hand and then gesture to where the other person should sit. If you are being welcomed, accept the hand that is offered and wait to be shown where to sit.

This process sounds formal and studied, but in fact usually happens quite naturally. We are used to the ritual of shaking hands on meeting and parting. We exchange brief eyebrow-raises in acknowledgement of each other's presence. Lean slightly forward, maintain eye contact, smile, and respond to the signals that you receive.

Shaking Hands

One of the origins of the handshake is said to be the gesture our ancestors exchanged when they wanted to show that they were not carrying a weapon. There is no threat or anxiety when someone can see your open palm. We form an impression of someone from the way that he or she shakes hands. A firm handshake is thought to be a sign of strength and honesty, especially when it is accompanied with steady eye contact and a warm smile. If you misjudge the strength of your handshake and deliver a bone-crushing squeeze you may be perceived as dominant and aggressive. A weak handshake, or one in which only the fingertips make contact, may be seen to indicate ineffectiveness and negativity, and could suggest that the offer of communication is insincere. A damp palm could be seen as indicating nervousness.

However, be careful not to use the handshake as the basis of your judgement of someone's personality and intentions.

A too strong handshake, or one that encloses the other's hand, or a double-handed shake, could be offered for a number of reasons:

- Being unaware of your strength.
- Nervousness.
- Enthusiasm.
- Desire to communicate sincerity.
- Eagerness to seem effective.

A weak handshake may be offered for any of the following reasons:

- The person is physically strong, and does not want to grip too hard.
- The need to protect the hands because of someone's job or profession – for example, a musician, a surgeon, an artist, a hand model.
- Embarrassment because of sticky or damp palms.
- A physical condition, such as arthritis.
- Not expecting to shake hands.

Handshakes and power

Putting the hand over the other person's hand with the palm down can indicate a wish to dominate (Figure 5). This gesture shows a desire to take control. If you offer your hand with the palm up, you are indicating that you accept the other person's dominance.

An effective and satisfying handshake is firm but not too strong, in which each person's palm is clasped in the same way and the hands are pumped up and down with equal vigour.

Figure 5 *Dominant handshake*

Eye Contact

Eye contact is a familiar aspect of non-verbal communication. Many of us who have few developed ideas about other aspects of body language have consciously or unconsciously acquired beliefs about the messages given by someone's way of looking at other people. Maybe this is because the signals given by the eyes, the windows of the soul, are central to communication in all our personal encounters. The pupils of the eye send messages that we cannot consciously control and to which we unconsciously respond. When we see something that we find attractive or interesting the pupils of our eyes dilate, becoming larger (Figure 6a), and when we respond to stimuli that arouse feelings such as anger or hostility, our pupils contract, becoming smaller and more 'beady' (Figure 6b). Without realizing it, we pick up and respond to these signals. Just as our pupils dilate when we are looking at someone or something that pleases us, so others are inclined to like us when our pupils are enlarged, and to feel less warm towards us if our pupils are contracted.

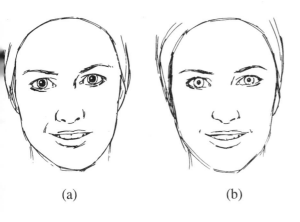

(a)   (b)

Figure 6 *Pupils dilating and contracting*

Eye contact and the pattern of communication

Activity 17 may well indicate that you associate poor eye contact with negative qualities. Eye contact is so central to the process of communication that when it is lacking or inappropriate we feel uncomfortable and ill at ease, and we are inclined to distrust someone who avoids looking us in the eye. There are certain patterns and rules that apply to the way that eye signals are used in communication, and if we get the rules wrong, for example by using too much or too little eye contact, other people are inclined to find us lacking credibility, not likeable and even untrustworthy.

The general pattern, as observed by Michael Argyle, is that people in conversation look at each other for between 30 per cent and 60 per cent of the time. Any longer than that can be seen as unsettling, embarrassing or threatening, associated not so much with workplace encounters as with the deeper personal involvement of lovers gazing into each other's eyes or enemies glaring at each other in preparation for hostilities. Eye contact of less frequency is interpreted as indicating qualities such as insincerity, or attitudes such as lack of interest.

It is customary for us to look at someone less when we are speaking than when we are listening. When we are talking, we maintain eye contact for about 40 per cent of the time. We do not gaze fixedly at the other person, but glance away momentarily as we think of the next point, or search for a word and then resume eye contact for a short while. When we are listening, we maintain more consistent eye contact, for about 75 per cent of the time. Looking more steadily than this at the person speaking can seem over-intent or staring, and less eye contact than this amount will be seen to indicate boredom or distraction.

Judging the right degree of visual contact is a matter of skill and practice. Looking at the person to whom you are speaking is vital for

ACTIVITY 17: What eye contact says about a person

Check out your own feelings about the messages conveyed by our use of eye signals. Put the following characteristics under the appropriate headings of 'Good eye contact' and 'Poor eye contact'. You could add your own ideas.

Untrustworthy	Aloof	Truthful	Superior
Paying attention	Sincere	Confident	Submissive
Trying to hide something	Shifty	Skilful	Assertive
Dishonest	Interested	Informed	Threatening
Friendly	Respectful	Impolite	

Good eye contact   *Poor eye contact*

_____

_____

_____

_____

_____

_____

building communication and rapport. As you speak, you need to be aware of the other's understanding and responses. However, if your glances are too short and too frequent you may create a jumpy and unsettled atmosphere. Try to hold the person's gaze for a few seconds before glancing away, then make your next eye contact last a little longer. As a listener, it can be difficult to maintain visual contact without getting into a fixed stare. Try to focus your gaze on the upper half of the face, and remember to respond with head and facial movements. Your eyes will alter as you respond – creasing as you smile, or opening wide as you show surprise or interest. Not only will this demonstrate that you are paying attention, but it will help you to feel and seem more natural.

ACTIVITY 18: Frequency of eye contact

Try this observation exercise. Watch two people in conversation and monitor the amount of eye contact made by the speaker and by the listener. How far does the pattern match the description above? Can you tell anything about the nature of the conversation from the frequency and type of eye contact?

_____

_____

_____

_____

_____

Different patterns of eye contact

With strangers

In some situations different rules of eye contact apply. We avoid meeting the gaze of others on public transport, for example. In situations where we are crowded together with strangers we deal with the fact that we are in close physical proximity to (or even touching) people we don't know by looking away and not meeting their eyes. This eliminates feelings of threat or embarrassment. Even in the lift at work people who know each other by sight still adhere to this rule, looking straight ahead and not at each other. As with most aspects of non-verbal communication,

deviation from this unwritten rule causes awkwardness and even alarm. Those whose behaviour does not conform to the accepted code are perceived as lacking in social awareness.

With colleagues

There are certain circumstances in which people tend not to look at each other much when they are speaking.

Scene 7: Sara and Niamh in conversation

Sara and Niamh are by the water cooler, deep in conversation. They are standing side by side with their heads inclined towards each other, and each nods in response to what is being said, but they do not engage in direct eye contact.

What would you infer about their relationship and the nature of the conversation? Tick the relevant boxes:

(a) They do not like each other. ☐

(b) One or both of them is shy. ☐

(c) One is the other's boss. ☐

(d) They are talking about something that is intimate, awkward or embarrassing. ☐

In fact, any one – or all – of the above could be true. In certain situations, such as those described, we may avoid eye contact, which is fine if there is mutual acceptance that this is appropriate. However, communication in these circumstances will be less effective if one of the people involved would like more eye contact.

How to encourage eye contact

Of course, you cannot force someone to look at you. What you *can* do is use a combination of verbal and non-verbal behaviour to bring about a change in at least the direction of their gaze.

Think about why the person is avoiding looking at you. It could be that he or she is shy, or feels awkward. The lack of eye contact could indicate coldness or unfriendliness, or it could be that the person is bored. Possibly the person disagrees with or does not understand what you are saying. You could find out more by asking a question, which should also have the effect of causing the person to look in your direction, at which point you can move if necessary so that you can meet their gaze. Moving your position so that you are sitting or standing closer or further away should also bring about a change. You can direct someone's gaze by pointing – for example, at a document or a board – then move your finger or pointer towards your own eyes, so that the person will look at them.

Some uses of eye contact

Regulating the flow of conversation

Awareness of people's eye movements can help to keep an interaction going without awkward pauses or inappropriate interruptions. Making eye contact with someone is a way of beginning an interaction and inviting the other person to communicate with us. During the conversation, when someone glances away do not assume that they have finished speaking. We tend to look upwards when we come to the end of what we are saying, and give a short glance to check the other's reaction. This gives an indication to other people that it is their turn to speak.

Communicating feelings and attitudes

Making appropriate eye contact with someone indicates friendliness, confidence and the willingness to communicate. Inappropriate eye contact may be associated with characteristics and attitudes that may or may not be those that you intend to convey.

The intimidating stare

Some people make use of a long, steady gaze in order to threaten or intimidate. Even if your intention is not to exert power, this is how such eye contact will be perceived by others. When you are on the receiving end of this kind of aggressive stare, your discomfort may cause you to break the gaze by dropping your eyes. This will be seen as a gesture of submission, indicating that you are giving in to the other's domination.

Scene 8: Sally feels intimidated

'I want to talk to you about the reception area,' Lorna says to Sally. 'We need it to be kept tidier throughout the day. It's fine in the morning, but after a few people have been in and out it looks really scruffy. Any ideas?' She looks at Sally steadily.

'Um . . .' Sally looks around the area, then

back at Lorna. Lorna is still watching her. Sally begins to feel uncomfortable, as if she personally has made it untidy. 'I suppose we could take it in turns to leave the desk and straighten things up.' She looks back at Lorna, whose gaze does not flicker. Sally drops her eyes, feeling intimidated.

The shifting glance

Not meeting someone's eyes can indicate that something is being hidden. It can also indicate shame or embarrassment. In some situations, nervousness or tension might cause your gaze to flicker sideways or up and down, then back to the speaker's face. Try to control your eye movements so that you meet the person's gaze for a few seconds, then speak yourself. As you speak, it will be natural for you to glance away, and you will feel less awkward and more in control of your gaze.

Scene 9: Julie covers up

Darren has promised to send a customer a replacement part, but is surprised to find that it is out of stock. The suppliers of the part are usually very reliable and respond quickly to requests.

'I thought you said you had ordered a new supply?' he asks Julie.

Julie does not meet his eyes, but looks to the side as she answers. 'I did,' she says. She glances at him and looks away again.

Darren feels that Julie is hiding something. Her body language indicates discomfort, and her refusal to meet his eyes directly suggests that she is hiding something. Darren does not jump to conclusions, but his observations mean that he will have to find out exactly what has happened before he contacts the suppliers.

The sideways look

Looking at someone sideways conveys an attitude of suspicion, doubt or hostility. Even if your words express agreement, your look implies rejection.

Scene 10: Naomi looks out of the corner of her eye

Rachel needs someone to be responsible for the new window display. Her first choice for this task is Lance, but he points out to Rachel that he will be on holiday at that time. Rachel decides to ask Naomi, who is fairly new to the job, but has shown ability. When Rachel asks her, Naomi does agree to take the assignment, but her body is turned away from Rachel, and she looks at her from out of the corner of her eye rather than meeting Rachel's gaze.

In this case, Rachel hears Naomi's verbal agreement but does not notice her contradictory body signals. She later discovers that Naomi knows that she was not the first to be asked and is annoyed about it. Rachel has lost this opportunity of discovering more about Naomi's personality and attitude. If Rachel had picked up the signals, she might have chosen to ask Naomi what was bothering her, and they might have been able to discuss the matter further.

ACTIVITY 19: Reading someone's glances (see Scene 10)

(a) What might Rachel deduce from Naomi's eye signals? Think of several possible answers:

1 _____

2 _____

3 _____

(b) How could Rachel's observation of Naomi's non-verbal message lead to effective communication between the two of them?

1 _____

2 _____

3 _____

Open and Closed Body Language

A characteristic of effective body language is its openness. By keeping your gestures away from your body you indicate that you have nothing to hide, and you show acceptance of others and a willingness to interact with them.

Barrier positions

If you fold your arms or cross them around your body, you will be seen as being defensive. Your arms form a protective guard in front of you, as if you are responding to an attack. This is the position we sometimes assume when we disagree with what is being said, and are not going to budge from our point of view.

Sometimes we adopt a modified version of this gesture by putting one arm across the body, a position that can be seen to communicate nervousness or lack of self-confidence. Another way of creating a protective barrier is to carry something like a bag or a file in front of us, almost like a shield. However, this habit could just be a practical way of protecting ourselves from people who may bump into or brush up against us.

A barrier can also be created if the hands are held high in front of the body, with the fingers intertwined. This position implies a negative or defensive attitude.

Your legs, too, can be crossed in what may be

ACTIVITY 20: The effect of eye contact

Choose a few encounters at work in which you can practise making eye contact. You might choose a conversation with your boss, or greeting someone in the corridor, or explaining a procedure to a co-worker. In each case, make a point of looking at them as much as you can, without making them feel uncomfortable. At the end of the day, make a note of each encounter and how you felt. You could use some of the following words to describe your reactions:

Embarrassed	Awkward
In control	Energized
Connected	Effective
Confident	Friendly

Person	*Situation*	*How I felt*
1		
2		
3		

Effective eye contact will convey confidence and trustworthiness. It will enable you to form good working relationships, and will earn you a reputation for openness and sincerity.

---

seen as a position conveying defensiveness or negativity. Locking your ankles together, or locking one foot around the other leg, suggests that you are feeling tense or uncomfortable.

Opening up

Being in a barrier position affects the way that you feel. It is difficult to feel open and relaxed if your limbs are tensely locked and intertwined.

Figure 7 *Arms creating barriers*

By changing your position, you can bring about a change in your mental state.

Scene 11: Simon unwinds

Mina is explaining a new working procedure to Simon. Simon has his arms folded high up on his chest and his legs are crossed. This position, together with his frown and slight shakes of the head, tells Mina that Simon is not responding positively to the proposed change.

Simon himself becomes aware of his bodily position. He uncrosses his arms and adopts a more open posture. He finds that he can now listen more objectively to Mina's explanation. You can encourage someone to adopt a more open posture by doing something that requires the person to unlock their arms or legs. You

Figure 8 *Locked legs*

could try handing them something to look at, or asking them to hand you something, or offering them a drink. If you want to bring about a total change in someone's posture you could try suggesting something that means walking to another area.

Signals of Power

There are certain postures and mannerisms that are seen to indicate a superior or patronizing attitude, and to be ways of asserting power and position. Sometimes this behaviour is seen as aggressive.

Ways of sitting

Sitting with the leg over one arm of the chair may in some contexts be a casual relaxed position, but in most work situations such a position communicates extreme self-confidence or superiority over the other person. This is a very masculine pose, which is not often used by women. Another position that suggests dominance is straddling the seat of the chair using its back as a prop and a shield. A sense of superiority is conveyed when someone sits with the ankle of one leg resting on the knee of the other leg with the arms clasped behind the back of the neck (Figure 9).

Ways of standing

Towering over someone can appear threatening, as can an exaggeratedly upright stance. A pose

37

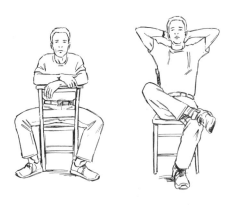

Figure 9 *Postures suggesting dominance or superiority*

other person. This kind of masked aggression is shown through gestures such as over-long eye contact, patting the arm or shoulder, or a too-friendly tone of voice. Other indications of manipulative intention are exaggerated displays of sincerity, such as studiedly open gestures.

Signs of Weakness

You may be seen as weak and easily pushed around if your body language sends submissive signals. Slumped posture, fidgeting, a hesitant tone of voice, and reluctance to make eye contact may be interpreted as indications of submissiveness. You might smile when you feel angry, suggesting that you back away from conflict or confrontation.

that indicates superior status is standing tall with the hands clasped behind the back and the head held high. Other postures that can indicate superiority are standing with hands on hips with the elbows jutting out and, in certain situations, maintaining a still posture.

Gestures and mannerisms

Folded arms can give a confrontational impression, as can habits such as pointing a finger. Fist clenching can show hostility, and moving in too close to someone can be an aggressive action.

Covered-up Aggression

Some types of body language imply friendship, but in fact indicate a desire to manipulate the

Assurance and Confidence

Developing the kind of body language that displays confidence in yourself, and respect for yourself and others, will help you to manage work situations effectively. Open body gestures, posture that is upright but relaxed, steady eye contact and clear hand gestures are examples of assertive non-verbal signals.

Show interest in the person to whom you are talking by keeping your whole body turned in their direction. The direction in which our feet point shows the focus of our attention. If your body is twisted so that your trunk faces the other person and your feet point outwards you are indicating that your interest is elsewhere. Keep your arms by your sides, away from your body. Do not put your hands near your face, or fiddle with items of clothing (Figure 10).

Figure 10 *Open postures*

Listening

Many work situations require that you listen attentively. You may have to listen to instructions, ideas, feedback, complaints, suggestions and so on. The ability to listen effectively is a skill that you can develop, and one that will be of great benefit in all areas of your working life, enabling you to build and maintain good interpersonal relationships and to take in information accurately and sensitively.

The important thing is to be seen to be listening. If you are talking to someone who looks the other way as you speak, you probably feel that he or she is not listening to you, no matter what is said. Listening must not only take place, but must be seen to take place.

Paying attention

You show that you are listening by the kinds of non-verbal signals that you give, and by the way that you respond to the body language of the person to whom you are talking.

ACTIVITY 21: Assertive bodytalk

What kind of assertive body language would you use in each of these situations?

(a) Telling someone that you cannot finish a task:

Posture _____

Gestures _____

Facial expression _____

Tone of voice _____

(b) Asking someone for help with a task:

Posture _____

Gestures _____

Facial expression _____

Tone of voice _____

Showing that you are receptive and available

Your behaviour might give the message that you are too busy and preoccupied to listen attentively. If you always seem to be in a hurry and doing several things at once, and if your acknowledgement of your co-workers and your interaction with them is cursory, you may be indicating a lack of interest in them. When you are in a situation that requires attentive listening, the perceptions that others have of you may be a barrier.

Scene 12: Douglas doesn't listen (1)

Rosina wants to talk to Douglas about the difficulties she is having with a particular client. She feels that it will be difficult to get his attention as he always gives the impression of being too busy to be bothered with people. When Douglas rushes into the office with his usual frown and brief nod and good morning in her direction, she gets up from her desk and says, Douglas, I would like to speak to you sometime today about . . .'

ACTIVITY 22: Signs of not listening

Look at these examples of the kind of behaviour that may be interpreted as showing that someone is not listening. Put a tick in the box for each one that you know applies to you. (If you are not sure, ask someone appropriate for feedback.)

Fidgeting ☐

Looking at your watch ☐

Playing with your hair ☐

Looking around the room ☐

Fiddling with a pen or similar item ☐

Shifting about ☐

Looking sideways at your computer screen ☐

Doodling ☐

Add your own examples:

_____ ☐

_____ ☐

_____ ☐

_____ ☐

Douglas is already halfway through the door, speaking on his phone. He turns his head in Rosina's direction, looks at his watch and nods.

Rosina is going off the idea of talking to him. He has arranged a time for them to meet, but she feels that he will not really listen to what she has to say.

Position and posture

How you sit or stand when you are listening is affected by, and can affect, the nature of the communication. Keeping a desk or a table between you could create a barrier that might prevent people from opening up and speaking freely, or it could underline the formality of a situation. If you are standing, a face-to-face posture shows that you are engaged with the person speaking and do not want to be interrupted. If you stand at right angles, your position suggests that you are open to interruption. Keep your body posture open and relaxed. Lean slightly towards the other person, but be careful not to invade his or her space.

Eye contact and facial expression

Maintain good eye contact in order to demonstrate your attention and to pick up the other person's facial expressions. Give non-verbal signals that show you are tuning in to what is being said. If someone is speaking very seriously about an issue, it would be most offputting if you listened with a smile. Make your facial expressions appropriate to what is being said – smile when your speaker is amused about something, look sober if he or she is expressing concern.

Body movements

Respond by giving little nods to show that you are taking in what is being said, and back these up with listening noises' such as mmm'. If you are puzzled by what someone says, or would like to hear more, tilt your head slightly to one side with a little lift of your eyebrows. Change your posture to reflect shifts in the conversation – lean forward or back to show that you recognize a significant point, or take a more casual position if the tone becomes lighthearted.

Listen for the whole message

Listen to the emotional content of what is being said as well as the actual words spoken. Someone's voice will indicate strength of feeling by becoming louder or more intense. Our gestures become more agitated when we are worked up about something. In general, facial expressions reveal what we are feeling and our gestures and movements show how strongly we feel it.

Scene 12: Douglas doesn't listen (2)

Rosina starts to tell Douglas about the problems with their client. Douglas drums a finger on the table as he listens, and his foot moves up and down.

'So you're saying that they keep changing their mind at the last minute?' He glances at the clock. 'That reminds me, I must chase up Ben today. Don't worry, we'll let it go this time, and give them a deadline for next month. That's sorted, then.'

'Fine.' Rosina shifts in her chair and looks down.

Douglas feels that he has dealt with the problem. Rosina feels that part of her problem has been dealt with, but that she was not able to say what is really on her mind. She is worried about the way that she is handling this particular client and thinks that they might take their custom elsewhere. Douglas does not notice Rosina's signs of anxiety. If he had listened in a different way, he would have noticed her body language and could have picked up the important long-term issues implicit in what Rosina was saying.

Becoming distracted

Sometimes physical distractions make it difficult to stay focused on what someone is saying. When you realize that you are losing concentration because of noise, or because you are hungry or have a headache, or because you are physically uncomfortable, don't just keep going. You may be in danger of focusing on the distraction, and letting it become an excuse for not listening.

Identify what the distraction is, and see what you can do about it. It might mean moving to a quieter area, or somewhere warmer or cooler. You might need to have a drink of water.

Do what you can to keep the flow of the conversation going. If it is impossible to deal with what is getting in the way, try to tune it out. Direct all your concentration towards the other person. Imagine that the two of you are enclosed in a soundproof bubble.

ACTIVITY 23: Better listening (see Scene 12)

(a) In what ways is Douglas not an effective listener?

(b) What changes could he make?

What he does	*What he could do*
1 _____	1 _____
2 _____	2 _____
3 _____	3 _____
4 _____	4 _____
5 _____	5 _____

ACTIVITY 24: Becoming an effective listener

Think of an occasion when you will be in the role of listener. Think about the kind of body language you will use, and what non-verbal signals you will watch for:

Situation _____

Body language I will use _____

_____

Body language signals I will look for in the other person _____

_____

43

Space and Territory

The way that we handle our environment and the space around us communicates something about our personality and attitudes. Your physical space at work, whether it is a desk, an office, a counter, a machine, a laboratory, a studio, a cubicle or whatever, can make a statement about the kind of person you are and how you relate to your co-workers both socially and in terms of the power and authority hierarchy in your workplace.

You also have personal space – that is, the kind of invisible bubble that surrounds each of us and protects us from intrusion. Our perception of the space that we and others occupy is determined by our cultural and social conditioning, which explains why different cultures and nationalities have different ideas about what is an acceptable interpersonal distance. How you deal with your own personal space and that of others is an important aspect of your personal communication style.

Personal space

Edward Hall (who wrote *The Silent Language*) coined the word *proxemics* (the study of space used when communicating) to describe aspects of how we relate to our personal space. There is an area of space around us that we claim as our own. We welcome certain people into this space, and keep others outside it. If our sense of space is violated, by someone being more distant or more close than is appropriate to our relationship with them, we may feel threatened and unsettled. The distance we maintain can express our feelings – we choose to move closer to someone we like, and to move further away from someone we dislike or with whom we do not feel comfortable.

Up close

This is the most intimate zone, the distance at which we can touch or be touched. This space ranges from about 6 to 18 inches (15 to 45 centimetres), and only certain people are welcomed into it.

Pretty personal

This is the arm's length distance, representing the space at which we can, for example, shake hands with others. The distance we maintain here is between 18 inches and 4 feet (46 centimetres to 1.2 metres).

Social space

In most everyday encounters we stand at a distance of about 4 to 12 feet (1.2 to 3.6 metres). We feel comfortable maintaining this space when we deal with work colleagues and people we know in other particular contexts.

Keep your distance

This public zone extends outwards from about 12 feet (3.6 metres). This is the distance between strangers.

Your physical workspace

The way that you organize your workspace gives an impression of your personality and your attitude to work. There is a balance to be struck between what feels comfortable and appropriate to you, and the expectations and perceptions of others.

ACTIVITY 25: Appropriate distances

How do you react when someone misjudges the appropriate distance? Think of a couple of occasions when this has happened. If you like, you could choose situations that you have observed in others:

Situation	Distance	Reaction	Effect on communication

(a) _____

_____

(b) _____

_____

Scene 13: Tamsin's messy work area

Tamsin's work area is cluttered and messy, and she likes it that way. She claims that she can find anything she needs within seconds, and that what may seem disorganized to other people is in fact a sign of creative chaos. However, others receive the impression that Tamsin's work will be sloppy, and are reluctant to trust her with important projects.

Entering Someone's Space

Going into a room

When you go into a room you are entering into someone else's space and territory. The way in which you enter gives signals about you and your relationship with, and attitude to, the other person. If your status is lower than his or hers you are likely to hover near the door until you are invited to come nearer. If you are of equal status you will go right up to the desk. One of the 'power games' sometimes played is to keep people standing at the door, or even outside it, in order to reinforce their lower status.

Getting attention

Approaching a group

When you go up to a group of people, you should be aware that you are entering their space. If this is done insensitively people are likely to feel invaded and annoyed, as *you* may have felt when someone has 'barged in'. At the same time, you need to get close enough for them to realize that you are there and want to speak with them. Approach the group until you are within the

45

social distance zone, close enough to be noticed, then catch someone's eye as if you are asking to be allowed in further. When you receive the reassurance of a smile or a nod, or continued eye contact, you can move closer.

Watch the direction in which people's bodies and feet are pointing. If they are turned away from you, with their feet pointing towards each other, they are indicating that they do not wish to welcome you into the group.

Approaching an individual

When you need to interrupt someone who is working, do not go right up to the person but keep on the edge of his or her personal space. Do not lean forward with any part of your body, and do not hover without speaking. Say something to announce your presence so that the person does not feel startled. If a woman is approached from behind she may experience a brief moment of panic, so in this kind of situation try to approach from the front, or move round so that you are facing her. Men tend to see face-on approaches as threatening, so try to go up to a man from the side.

Space, Power and Status

We use space and size to indicate importance. Big offices and desks, large cars, spacious living areas – all are taken as indicators of status. People who lack self-confidence try to minimize the amount of space that they occupy, as if apologizing for their presence, while those who wish to make an impression claim the maximum space around them. This can be done by sitting with arms and legs spread out, or seizing space by distributing personal items across the claimed area.

Invading space

The invasion of your personal or physical space can be annoying and, at the worst, intimidating. Sometimes people will do this as a deliberate display of power. It may be through little actions like fiddling with or helping themselves to your personal items, or perching on the edge of your desk. Looking over someone's shoulder is an invasion of space.

Be alert to the ways in which people at work mark out their own territory. It could be through the strategic placing of a jacket over the back of a chair, or leaving a newspaper on a desk or table. Dusting surfaces, touching merchandise, rearranging items, or just picking them up and putting them down are all ways of marking individuals' work territory. Be prepared for a hostile reaction if you do not notice these markers and inadvertently invade someone's space.

4

The Way That You Say It

When we speak, our voices communicate much more than words. Non-verbal aspects such as the pace and pitch of our voices, the stress we put on certain words, the way that we use pauses, and the tone in which we speak all help to communicate our meaning. It is alarmingly easy to create an impression that we do not intend by getting these aspects of what is called *paralanguage* just slightly wrong. You may have had the experience of sounding sarcastic when you did not mean to, or of trying to sound authoritative only to have your message undermined by a squeaky breathy voice. It is possible to alter the sound of your voice to help you to control the impression you create.

Your Posture and Your Voice

The way that you stand affects the way that you speak. A relaxed, balanced, upright posture is the first step to an effective speaking voice. If your vocal instruments are cramped because you are slumped or slouching, the sounds that your voice produces will be strained.

Efficient Breathing

Correct breathing is an essential part of voice control. The key to good breathing is the way that you breathe out. If you concentrate on breathing in you might just inhale air and try to hold it, which could result in a light-headed feeling from the extra oxygen, and in a breathy uncontrolled voice when you exhale and speak.

ACTIVITY 26: Breathing out

Try this after work – it will help you to relax as well as helping your voice control. Lie on your back with one hand on your abdomen and one on your chest. Breathe in, keeping your chest still and feeling your abdomen and lower ribs expand. As you breathe out, make sure that your chest is still and that your abdomen muscles do the work. Concentrate on the out breath, making it last as long as you can, until all the air is expelled.

Speaking Clearly

You might think that you are speaking clearly, but your listener might in fact find it difficult to distinguish your words. Straining to understand what someone is saying can be tiring and annoying. Be careful not to slur your words together or lose the sound at the ends of words. Make a particular effort with consonants such as p, d and g, especially when they occur at the ends of words. If you articulate these sounds clearly you will sound more definite and authoritative.

Volume

How loudly or softly we speak affects the way that our words are interpreted. Loud speech is associated with strong emotions, such as anger or excitement, and those who speak softly may be perceived as lacking confidence and certainty.

Try to vary the volume at which you speak, and match it to the particular circumstances. Sometimes deliberately lowering the voice can be an effective way of emphasizing your words and of gaining someone's attention. It can also be an indirect way of showing aggression – speaking in exaggeratedly quiet tones can sound threatening or over-controlling.

Tone

The tone of voice that someone uses can reinforce the words that are spoken or contradict them. Sometimes we deliberately mismatch our words and tone – when we are being sarcastic or ironic, for example. On these occasions other body language signals, such as facial expression and gestures, make our intention clear. Sometimes the mismatch is caused through a lack of awareness of the tone that we are using.

ACTIVITY 27: Same words, different tone
The same words spoken in different tones can convey entirely different meanings. Try saying 'Of course I will do that' in different tones of voice:

> Friendly
> Sarcastic
> Eager
> Reassuring
> Threatening
> Efficient
> Offhand
> Confident

Pace and Pause

Pace describes the speed and rhythm of our speech. Our normal rate of speaking in public is about 125 words per minute, but this will vary according to our natural tendency and the context in which we are speaking. It is a common practice to speak too quickly when we are nervous (although in this situation some people speak in slow and stumbling phrases), and to speak too slowly when we want to sound impressive.

Use pauses for emphasis, and to give the other person time to take in what you are saying.

Pitch

Most of us have a pitch range of about two octaves, with men's voices being slightly lower than women's because their vocal chords are longer. We all have a natural pitch level that we use most frequently, with the ability to move higher or lower. If you do not use this ability, but instead speak on the same note the whole time, your voice will sound boring and communication will be less effective than if you vary its pitch.

People do tend to make assumptions about personality traits from the pitch of someone's voice. A low-pitched voice can give the impression of authority and control, whereas if your natural pitch is high, you might come across as lightweight or emotional.

The upward and downward inflections of our voice create a pitch pattern, which can reinforce or undermine the impression we want to create.

Scene 14: Peter changes pitch

Peter realizes that the instructions he gives are not always carried out within the time scale that he states. There does not seem to be any reason for this. He discusses the matter with a friend, who points out that Peter's voice goes up at the end of his sentences. This rising inflection gives what he says a hesitant air, and suggests that he is asking if it will be all right rather than stating that it has to be done. For a more authoritative effect, he should end on a falling pitch tone.

ACTIVITY 28: Different pitches

Try saying the sentence 'I would like you to deliver it on Thursday' in two ways. First, speak the last word with a rising inflection. Then say the sentence again with a downward inflection on the last word. Which sounds more definite?

Emphasis

Emphasis is a way of making words stand out in a spoken sentence. When its use is well judged, it makes your meaning clear and adds force to your communication. If you emphasize the wrong word, you can send a message entirely different from the one that you intended.

ACTIVITY 29: Placing emphasis

Repeat the sentence below out loud, emphasizing the word in italics in each example:

(a) The *order* was not received yesterday.
   This implies that the order was not received yesterday, but that something else was.

(b) The order was not received *yesterday*.
   This implies that the order was not received yesterday, but at some other time.

49

You can create a sense of trust and confidence if you put a slight emphasis on positive words rather than negative ones. This may be helpful when presenting ideas, or dealing with clients.

ACTIVITY 30: Listen to your own voice

What is the pace, the tone and the rhythm of your own way of speaking? Think of two occasions when you would like to vary your style of speech:

Situation   *How I would like to speak*

(a) _____   _____

 _____   _____

(b) _____   _____

 _____   _____

Scene 15: Rita's interview

Do you remember Rita and her job interview (Scene 4)? In her interview at the public relations company, she speaks as she does at her present workplace. Her tone is brisk and businesslike, and her voice sounds crisp. This strikes a jarring note in the new environment. She comes across as efficient – but cold. In this different field of work, a warmer, more friendly tone is appropriate.

A little way into the meeting Rita becomes aware of the fact that she is speaking in a different way from the people who are interviewing her. She modulates her tone and speaks more slowly, picking up the rhythms of the other voices.

Rita realizes that although she can do nothing about the fact that she is dressed inappropriately for this particular situation, she can alter the way that she speaks in order to create more positive communication.

Body Language and the Telephone

When speaking on the phone, you create an impression entirely through your voice. The listener cannot see you, or your facial expressions and gestures. They cannot see what you are doing as you speak, or how you are reacting to what is being said. This throws enormous emphasis on to your voice and how you sound. We form impressions of people from their voices, getting a mental picture of what they look like and an idea of their personal characteristics.

People 'sound' tall, small, fat or thin. We say that people sound friendly, or warm, or brusque, or cold, having received these ideas from what they sound like as much as, or more than, from what has been said. You may have experienced the shock of meeting phone correspondents for the first time and finding that they do not look a bit like they sound!

ACTIVITY 31: What are they like?

Choose three people you speak to on the phone, but have never met. For each one, describe the impression you have formed through their voices of their physical characteristics and of their personalities. Circle a number on the continuum for each characteristic.

Person a _____

Voice

High	1	2	3	4	5	6	7	8	9	Low
Fast	1	2	3	4	5	6	7	8	9	Slow
Clear	1	2	3	4	5	6	7	8	9	Unclear
Jerky	1	2	3	4	5	6	7	8	9	Smooth

Characteristics

Friendly	1	2	3	4	5	6	7	8	9	Unfriendly
Warm	1	2	3	4	5	6	7	8	9	Cold
Helpful	1	2	3	4	5	6	7	8	9	Unhelpful
Tall	1	2	3	4	5	6	7	8	9	Short
Old	1	2	3	4	5	6	7	8	9	Young

Add your own examples

_____	1	2	3	4	5	6	7	8	9	_____
_____	1	2	3	4	5	6	7	8	9	_____
_____	1	2	3	4	5	6	7	8	9	_____

THE WAY THAT YOU SAY IT

Person b _____

Voice

High	1	2	3	4	5	6	7	8	9	Low
Fast	1	2	3	4	5	6	7	8	9	Slow
Clear	1	2	3	4	5	6	7	8	9	Unclear
Jerky	1	2	3	4	5	6	7	8	9	Smooth

Characteristics

Friendly	1	2	3	4	5	6	7	8	9	Unfriendly
Warm	1	2	3	4	5	6	7	8	9	Cold
Helpful	1	2	3	4	5	6	7	8	9	Unhelpful
Tall	1	2	3	4	5	6	7	8	9	Short
Old	1	2	3	4	5	6	7	8	9	Young

Add your own examples

_____	1	2	3	4	5	6	7	8	9	_____
_____	1	2	3	4	5	6	7	8	9	_____
_____	1	2	3	4	5	6	7	8	9	_____

Person c _____

Voice

High	1	2	3	4	5	6	7	8	9	Low
Fast	1	2	3	4	5	6	7	8	9	Slow
Clear	1	2	3	4	5	6	7	8	9	Unclear
Jerky	1	2	3	4	5	6	7	8	9	Smooth

Characteristics

Friendly	1	2	3	4	5	6	7	8	9	Unfriendly
Warm	1	2	3	4	5	6	7	8	9	Cold
Helpful	1	2	3	4	5	6	7	8	9	Unhelpful
Tall	1	2	3	4	5	6	7	8	9	Short
Old	1	2	3	4	5	6	7	8	9	Young

Add your own examples

_____	1	2	3	4	5	6	7	8	9	_____
_____	1	2	3	4	5	6	7	8	9	_____
_____	1	2	3	4	5	6	7	8	9	_____

Your telephone voice

Have you ever noticed that our voices change according to who we are speaking to? We have different ways of speaking to friends, family, work colleagues, bosses. In conversation with someone we know well, for example, our tone of voice is intimate and casual, whereas with someone more distant from us we sound more formal and removed. This is particularly obvious on the telephone, when we can be taken by surprise by a caller and have to adjust to the appropriate telephone voice. You may have heard people quickly change their vocal manner when they realize they are talking to a customer or their boss, and not a friend or family member.

ACTIVITY 32: Identifying phone voices

You could try this at work and at home. Listen for a few minutes to someone speaking on the phone, and see if you can correctly identify the person to whom he or she is talking. Try to tell from the tone, pitch and the pace of the voice, not from other clues! (The point is not to get the precise identity of the person, but to establish from the vocal characteristics the nature of the relationship.)

Create a picture with your voice when speaking on the phone

The people with whom you deal on the phone will form their own mental picture of you, just as you do of them. Identifying the vocal qualities that have led you to make certain judgements will help you to manage the impression that you create on the phone. Decide how you should sound. Do you need to convey your authority, or do you want your warm and friendly nature to be heard on the phone? Practise speaking in a way that conveys your personal characteristics.

Try some visualization here – imagine yourself as you want the person to see you. Keep in your mind an image of yourself as competent and efficient, or warm and friendly.

Posture and gestures when making phone calls

Your voice is affected by the way that you sit and stand. Your posture affects your breathing and alters your voice slightly, so that even though your listeners cannot see that you are slumped over a desk or bending down to pick up something as you speak, it is more than likely that they will hear a lack of energy or engagement in your voice. Sitting up straight or standing up will help to make your voice sound more positive and energetic and will help to create a professional impression.

ACTIVITY 33: Your impression on the phone

Choose three qualities that you would like to convey in your telephone voice. Identify the characteristics of your voice that will indicate these qualities:

Quality 1 _____

Vocal characteristics _____

Quality 2 _____

Vocal characteristics _____

Quality 3 _____

Vocal characteristics _____

Standing up when you are speaking on the phone is particularly helpful in situations where you need to increase your confidence. You will feel in a stronger position, and this will be reflected in your voice. Standing up can help you to make decisions, and it can also help to bring some vigour to your voice and focus your attention if you are feeling bored or your mind is wandering.

Gestures, of course, cannot be seen on the phone, but their impact can be felt in the way that you speak. When you are being, for example, forceful, or persuasive, use the same gestures that you would if you were speaking face to face.

This will reinforce your words and enhance the power of your communication.

Greetings and the phone

The way that you answer the phone at work creates a positive or negative impression. The tone of your voice can convey an attitude that may affect the rest of the conversation. Some people are unaware of how they come across when they answer the phone, while others deliberately cultivate a certain tone – for example, one that they think makes them sound busy, or one that is designed to put callers off.

ACTIVITY 34: Phone behaviour

What attitudes might be suggested by these examples of behaviour while speaking on the phone?

(a) Sitting with feet on the desk _____

(b) Personal grooming habits such as smoothing your hair _____

(c) Swivelling in the chair _____

(d) Doodling _____

(a) and (c) These positions may indicate that the speaker is feeling dominant and in control of the conversation.

(b) Preening gestures could suggest some romantic or sexual interest.

(d) Doodling might show boredom. On the other hand, some people find that it helps them to think.

As with every aspect of body language, do not interpret these signals in isolation. Remember that although you cannot be seen, the attitudes reflected in your actions and gestures while you are speaking may well leak out in your voice.

Pace of speaking on the phone

When you are waiting even a moment or two for someone to answer their phone, you have to adjust quickly to the sound of the person's voice. There may well be a moment when you are not fully tuned in to what is being said. When you answer your phone, it is sometimes a good idea to make the first thing you say fairly neutral, in case the caller misses a piece of information.

When you are tuned in to the other voice, try to pace it with your own. Listen to the speed at which he or she speaks, and pick up the pitch and the tone. Adjust your own voice accordingly – speed up or slow down a little, speak more loudly or more softly, at a higher or lower pitch. This will enable you to build up rapport with the other person, even though you cannot see each other. (There is more about this in Chapter 6.)

If you have to give complicated directions or costings over the phone, break up what you are saying into small chunks, and pause between each one.

Leakage of your feelings while on the phone

Do not assume that when you are speaking on the phone you can hide your real feelings and attitudes. You might have observed people on the phone using friendly and co-operative words while pulling faces and raising eyebrows to indicate that they are putting on an act. It is quite likely that the person on the other end of the line detects a lack of sincerity in the voice. The fact that our facial expressions cannot be seen and our working surroundings are invisible does not mean that we can relax our attention to body language. In fact, the lack of visual communication can increase our sensitivity to the impression created by the voice. That our voices can reveal more than we think they do is illustrated by the decision of some insurance companies in the United Kingdom to fit phone lines with lie detectors to identify fraudulent claims. When we lie, the tone and pitch of our voices change imperceptibly, and high-tech devices can pick up these vocal variations.

5

Reading the Signs

Picking up the non-verbal signals of groups of people is essential in many working situations. Those whose job entails observation, such as people who work in law enforcement or security, are trained in the accurate interpretation of crowd behaviour. Sometimes the safety of the public relies on their ability to identify body language that indicates the possibility of threatening or anti-social behaviour. In other fields of work, you can become more effective at your job through developing the ability to observe people's non-verbal signals. Any job that involves dealing with groups of people requires the accurate reading of body language. Teaching, lecturing and presenting, working in medical centres, public transport, theatres and cinemas, are just some of the areas of work in which picking up and responding to behavioural signals is essential to successful outcomes. In bars and restaurants, for example, staff who can respond to the needs of groups of customers through picking up aspects of their body language are likely to deliver better service and provide more customer satisfaction.

Observing Customers

Pace and timing in offering service

Scene 16: Josh learns some waiter techniques

Josh has just started work as a waiter in a busy restaurant. He is eager to give his customers the best possible service, and to contribute to their enjoyment of their meal with speedy and efficient attention. On his first night, a party of six sits at one of his tables. They order drinks, which he serves at once, and they pick up the menus. After a few minutes Josh goes over and asks if they are ready to order. To his surprise, they look rather irritated. At the end of the meal when they ask for the bill, once more they seem to be annoyed. Josh asks Pat, an experienced waiter, what he might have done wrong.

'You need to watch their body language,' Pat tells him. Some people want a little time to decide what to order because they are in the middle of a conversation. The party you were serving were chatting and laughing together, and you broke in. It would be better to wait until they are all actually reading the menu, or until you know that they have decided what they want.'

'How do I know that?' asks Josh.

'People put down the menu, and look up, or look round for their waiter. That is the ideal time to take their order. Just watch their body movements.'

'What about at the end, when they were sorting out the bill? I waited as they did it so that they could easily give me the payment.'

'Standing there might have made them feel under pressure. Also, they may feel a little awkward doing their sums and counting out money in front of someone else. You need to give them a bit of space.'

Pat goes on to tell Josh that he should avoid making eye contact with his customers until he is ready to deal with them, at which point the visual acknowledgement indicates that they will have his immediate attention.

Josh puts these ideas into practice, and his tips go up as he learns how to match his timing and pace to his customers' gestures and movements.

Eye techniques and customers

Josh also watches the way that Pat runs the bar, and learns how to use eye contact to assure waiting customers that he is attending to their needs.

Scene 17: Pat scans the bar

Pat is an experienced bar worker, who can deal swiftly and efficiently with a long queue of thirsty customers. His eyes are constantly scanning the people waiting, so that as he is attending to one person he can indicate who he will be serving next, and at the same time be taking money and pouring the next customer's drink.

Judging the customer's requirements

When you go into a shop, you are likely either to go straight to the counter or nearest selling point and ask for what you want, or you browse around, touching and picking up different items, or leafing through brochures and advertising material. As a customer, you will want attention from the sales staff at the appropriate moment. If you are approached too soon you might well feel pounced on and pressurized, but if you have to wait too long for attention, you might well feel irritated and may decide to take your custom elsewhere.

Scene 18: Gerri's customer

Gerri observes Marilyn as she comes into the clothes department. Marilyn is looking at a rack of dresses, fingering the material, and pulling out one or two to examine at arm's length. Gerri knows that it will be a mistake to invade Marilyn's space too early. Marilyn moves on and looks at other items, then goes back to the dresses. At this point Gerri approaches her and asks if she can help, and receives a positive response.

Eye messages and customers

Sometimes a sense of embarrassment prevents us from making appropriate eye contact with people who we know are being kept waiting, or who are in other ways not receiving good service.

Scene 19: The impatient queue

Susan is on the cash desk of a busy DIY store. The customer she is attending to wants an item that has to be collected from the stock room. While she is waiting for someone to bring the item, Susan is aware of the impatient body movements of the queue. People shift from side to side and raise their shoulders with expressions of exasperation. Susan feels uncomfortable and fixes her gaze on the counter, not looking up until the article is delivered.

Susan feels awkward because she does not know how to attend to both the current customer and those waiting. Her response to the signs of impatience is to pretend that she has not seen them. This behaviour is likely to cause more dissatisfaction.

Observing Groups in Your Workplace

In every workplace there are groups and factions. Some groups and individuals are friendly with each other but not with anyone else; others share loyalty but not friendship; others are locked into hostility and rivalry. You can learn a lot from watching the body signals of friendship groups in your workplace.

What makes the group tick

Careful observation will tell you a great deal about the nature of a particular group of colleagues. For example, you can spot who is the leader or most powerful member of the set. This is often the person to whom the others listen with nods of agreement, and who readily gains their attention. You might notice that other group members copy this person's gestures and positions, and that he or she tends physically to lead the way by going first. Once you have identified this, you have some idea of the pecking order within the group, and some idea of the group's values and attitudes. The person who has most influence with them is likely to embody the characteristics and approaches with which they identify or to which they aspire.

You can gain further insight into the group norms that operate by observing the choices that they make about behaviour and the use of space. A group that never uses the work canteen, for instance, but instead has breaks within its own area, is displaying its group identity. Such behaviour may show the closeness of the team, and could indicate an aloofness and distance from other groups.

Scene 20: Group leader

Maeve is a manager for a hospital trust. She notices that the technicians who work in the haematology laboratory form a close-knit group. They huddle together at breaks, forming a circle that excludes others. Rod appears to be the leader. He does not say a great deal, but when he speaks everyone in the group turns towards him and displays signs of attentive listening. Their facial expressions in these conversations display negativity and resentment, and their body movements become tense and aggressive.

Maeve checks out her observations through discussions with Rod and other individuals in the group. Everything Rod says expresses a cynical attitude to the way that the trust is run, and it appears that his views are those that the group has adopted as its own.

Maeve has discovered significant aspects of the group's behaviour and attitudes through her observation of their body language. She can now decide how to handle this situation.

ACTIVITY 36: Observing a group

Choose three groups of people at your place of work who are friends with one another. For each one, pick out the signs that identify the leader of the group. Notice the kinds of behaviour that indicate what the group is like.

	Group	Leader	How I know	Group characteristics
1				
2				
3				

Spotting alliances

Friendships between individuals are quite easily spotted. People will spend time together, showing an intimate use of space and making frequent eye contact. Their posture and gestures will be similar (see Chapter 6).

The same thing happens with groups of people. In some departments you will see that people dress in a similar way. For example, a group of women may signal that they identify with one another by wearing the same kinds of earrings; in another department it might be the done thing to wear scarves tied in a certain style. Quite often it is the leader or most powerful person in the group who sets the trend. Bonded groups at work will eat in the same places and laugh at the same things.

Using your observation skills to identify alliances will, at the very least, prevent you from putting your foot in it by, for example, criticizing someone without realizing that you are speaking to that person's strong supporter. Awareness of the group dynamics that operate in your particular place of work will help you to judge how you approach others and communicate effectively with them.

Scene 21: Mandy joins the group

Mandy has just joined the telesales team, and would like to be friendly with the group who have lunch together each day. They look as if they are good fun, and always come back laughing and joking. The problem is that they seem very established as a group, and rather off-putting to outsiders.

Mandy begins by staying on the edge of the group, and building rapport with them by matching the individuals' body language (see Chapter 6). The first time that she joins them for lunch she is careful to follow rather than take the lead, and she holds back from sitting down until everyone has taken their place. She knows that such a well-established group will have habits and rituals that she must respect if she wants to establish a good relationship with them. She makes sure that her posture and gestures are open, and neither defensive nor pushy, and she takes care not to invade anyone's space. At first she listens, showing attention and interest with her use of eye contact and facial responses. She notices that most of the laughter follows something that Wendy has said. Mandy begins to contribute gradually to the conversation. At this point she makes careful (but unobtrusive!) observations of the others' responses. When she sees that they listen to her without turning away or fidgeting, and that they make eye contact as she speaks, she feels accepted and able to make a greater contribution.

Mandy is now a part of the group, but she has not as yet taken any risks with her communication. She laughs at others' jokes, but does not make any herself. When she does come up with a quip about their supervisor's new hairstyle, she is pleased that everyone laughs, but she notices that Wendy's face tightens slightly, and that she smiles through closed, tight lips. Mandy realizes that Wendy may feel that her role as the most amusing one in the group is being threatened. Mandy's awareness of Wendy's leaked body signals heightens her understanding of the relation-ships within the group, and enables her to decide how she wishes her own role to be seen.

ACTIVITY 37: Joining a group

Pick a group at work that you would like to join. Begin by observing the group's behaviour and interactions, then plan how you will approach them.

Group members _____

Leader _____

Characteristic behaviour _____

Plan to join the group

Step 1 _____

_____

Step 2 _____

_____

Step 3 _____

_____

Danger Signs in Body Language

Careful observation of body language can alert you to situations in which you may want to take particular types of action. Non-verbal signals can communicate emotional states such as stress, tension and anger, and can also indicate when someone is covering up or not telling the truth.

Stress signals

You can learn to recognize stress symptoms in yourself and in others. Physical reactions to watch out for include a racing heart, breathless-ness, shaking or sweating, and going red or white in the face. If you find this happening to you at work, try some emergency short-term measures to bring your body back down to a calm state. If you can, go somewhere quiet. Relax each part of your body in turn and do some slow breathing. (You could try the breathing exercise in Chapter 7.) Use your mind to help you calm your body. Visualize a place and situation in which you feel calm. Imagine that you are in that place. Use all your senses to re-create the experience of feeling stress-free and totally relaxed. These techniques will help you to get through the day – but if you experience stress symptoms regularly, take a close look at what might be causing them. Your body is telling you that you may need to make some changes.

If a co-worker's body language shows significant changes, he or she could be suffering from stress. You might notice that someone starts talking much more loudly or softly, or walking much more quickly or slowly. The person might talk about a change in sleep patterns. Other indications that you might notice are body tension revealed through clenched hands, tapping fingers and nervous speech or laughter.

Do not jump to the conclusion that all such changes indicate stress. These body signs will be accompanied by changes in the person's emotional state and in his or her ability to think and concentrate.

The body talk of anger

The body language of anger is very similar to that of stress. You have probably experienced the pounding heart and tense muscles that accompany angry feelings. When you are dealing with someone who is angry, use the kind of body language that will help both you and the other person to become calm. The most important thing is not to seem aggressive. Shift your position if necessary so that you are not face to face in a confrontational position, and move so that you are both on the same level. Keep your gestures open and relaxed – do not clench your fists or point your finger.

Scene 22: The angry customer

Luke is furious because the supposedly fixed fault in his car has recurred. Before he says a word, it is clear to everyone in the garage workshop that he is very angry. He drums his fingers on the counter and looks round impatiently. His mouth and jaw are tight and his eyebrows are drawn together.

Brian is sitting behind the counter. He does not stand up or come round immediately, which may appear confrontational, but instead lets Luke talk. Brian sits upright with his head forward and a slight frown, which shows that he is acknowledging Luke's anger. He does not interrupt or argue, but gives little nods to show that he is taking in what Luke is saying. He comes from behind the counter and stands at a comfortable distance from Luke with his whole body turned towards him.

Brian speaks a little faster than he would normally, matching Luke's pace of speech, then gradually slows down. Luke's rate of speaking becomes less rapid. Brian makes a point of using Luke's name, and keeps his body language still and non-threatening.

Luke calms down, and they are able to discuss the problem.

Lies and Deception

The concepts of lying and deceiving are not always clear-cut, and ways of detecting and revealing falsehood through body language need to be applied with caution. Professionals concerned with law enforcement and safety and security are trained in different techniques of lie detection, in some cases backed up with technology such as electronic lie detectors. The ability to pick up clues in airport screening, for example, or in ensuring the security of buildings, is obviously of paramount importance. However, expert liars such as spies, criminals and confidence tricksters know the rules of body language, and practise the kinds of open gestures that convince others of their truthfulness and sincerity, while avoiding the signs most commonly associated with deception. This has led to the development of increasingly sophisticated devices to reveal when a suspect is lying. For example, a new kind of high-definition thermal imaging camera, trialled in 2002 by scientists from both the United Kingdom and the United States, can detect in liars a very slight blush, caused by the increased blood flow around the eyes that occurs from the stress created when someone is trying to disguise the fact that they are not telling the truth.

However, in the everyday workplace we have to rely on our observation of non-verbal and verbal behaviour to alert us to instances of deception. There are different degrees and types of deception. Deception can range from telling deliberate falsehoods in order to get a job, or to avoid being blamed for something, to exaggerating our successes or putting a positive gloss on something negative. Activity 38 will help you to focus on the truthfulness of your own behaviour and that of other people.

Someone who is not being entirely honest will often indicate this through body signals. On the occasions you have identified when you were aware that someone was not being completely honest it is likely that, consciously or subconsciously, you responded to gestures that indicated a lack of consistency with what was being said. Possibly, if your assumption that the person was lying was correct, you noticed a cluster of signals that made you aware of the person's discomfort. In this context, as in all others, there are very few pieces of non-verbal communication that can be read in isolation.

Some behaviours that could indicate lying

Hand-to-face gestures

It has been noted that when children tell lies, their hands fly to cover their mouths immediately afterwards. As adults, our instinctive behaviour is rather similar. When we have told a lie, or want to conceal the truth, we bring our hand up to our face as if to cover our mouths. Sometimes the hand forms a guard over the mouth, or else it by-passes the mouth and instead lightly rubs or touches the nose. Our instinct is to cover the

ACTIVITY 38: Degrees of deception

Think of situations at work in which you have been deceitful or less than completely honest:

A time when I:	Situation or context	What the purpose was	How I felt
– told a deliberate lie			
– falsified slightly			
– held back information			
– exaggerated			
– pretended not to understand			
– deliberately misunderstood			
– evaded an issue			

(continued)

READING THE SIGNS

Now apply the same behaviours to other people. Think about times when you knew that someone was behaving in one of these ways. How did you know that the person was not being honest?

A time when someone: *Situation or context*   *How I could tell*

– told a deliberate lie _____

_____

– falsified slightly _____

_____

– held back information _____

_____

– exaggerated _____

_____

– pretended not to understand _____

_____

– deliberately misunderstood _____

_____

– evaded an issue _____

_____

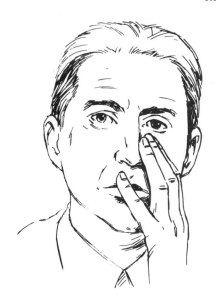

Figure 11 *Hand guarding the mouth*

mouth, but we try to control this give-away gesture, and the result is the nose rub (Figure 11).

In fact, the skin on the nose might actually itch. When we are under stress the skin does get hotter, and the nose might indeed feel tingly. Similarly, in the stressful situation of trying to pull the wool over someone's eyes, the increased blood flow makes our neck feel itchy. In response, we sometimes rub our neck, so revealing our discomfort, or divert attention by tugging or pulling at a collar or neck chain, so revealing that we are trying to disguise our discomfort!

Sometimes the body's response to stress may result in clearly visible blushing or sweating – which are possible indications that someone is not telling the truth.

ACTIVITY 39: Covering the mouth

Think of different reasons why someone with whom you are speaking might put a hand over their mouth:

1 _____

2 _____

3 _____

4 _____

How would you try to arrive at an accurate interpretation of the person's behaviour? _____

_____

Twitchy legs

The lower half of the body can reveal that someone is suffering from the pressure of trying to maintain a pretence. Increased movement of the lower limbs, such as shuffling feet or repeatedly crossing and uncrossing the legs, may be an indication that someone is not being truthful.

Voice give-aways

You may be able to tell from the way that someone speaks that he or she is trying to hide something. Variations in voice pitch and stutters or tremors may be indications of this, as may repeatedly clearing the throat, or even stopping talking altogether.

Responding to signs of deception

Once you have realized that someone is not telling the truth you need to decide how to respond. Your decision will depend on the context and on the nature of the falsehood.

ACTIVITY 40: Lies and small lies

Here are some ways that people being interviewed for a job might cover up the truth. Put them in what you consider to be their order of importance. You can do this by putting a number beside each one (1 = most important; 5 = least important):

Lying about a previous salary ☐

Exaggerating the importance of a previous job ☐

Falsifying qualifications ☐

Falsely claiming to have had experience of a certain area of work ☐

Pretending to enjoy working in a team ☐

Add your own ideas below:

_____ ☐

_____ ☐

_____ ☐

_____ ☐

Of course, you may think that each of the examples in Activity 40 is equally unacceptable. Nevertheless, you can choose whether you want to:

- ignore the lie;
- pretend to ignore the lie;
- confront the person with the falsehood;
- encourage the person to elaborate so that you can find out more.

Whatever strategy you choose, you can use your body language to affect the outcome.

Scene 23: Robert is evasive about his previous career

Vikram is interviewing Robert for a job as supervisor in the packaging department. So far Robert has answered his questions openly and confidently. Vikram moves on to discuss Robert's previous experience.

'Can you tell me something about managing the team at Lucas International?'

Robert clears his throat and does not respond as fluently as before. 'Well, I . . . er . . . let me see . . . I was there for three years and got on very well with everyone.' His hand goes up to his face and he shifts in his seat.

Vikram can see that Robert's foot is twitching. He thinks that Robert is hiding something, and feels that it is important to find out what it is. Vikram decides to adopt a confrontational approach to make Robert reveal what it is he is hiding. He leans forward into Robert's space and engages him in eye contact for a longer period than usual. 'I'd like to hear a bit more about your time at Lucas,' he says.

Robert goes red and says, 'There is not much more to say.' He clears his throat, and gives brief answers to Vikram's further questions.

Vikram makes some external enquiries before coming to a decision, and discovers that Robert left Lucas International under something of a cloud. Vikram's observations of Robert's non-verbal signals were accurate, and he used his own body language to show that he wanted to find out the truth.

Scene 24: At the doctor's surgery

Helen holds open the door for her last patient, Joe. Joe says that he has hurt his ankle playing football, and would like her to take a look at it. Helen deals with the ankle problem, and as Joe is doing up his shoe she asks him if there is anything else. Joe says that there isn't, but he looks uncomfortable.

'Are you sure?' Helen asks.

'Yes, I'm sure,' says Joe. He swallows hard and rubs his ear, and looks away from Helen.

Helen observes Joe's body language, and decides that she needs to encourage him to say what is on his mind. She pushes her chair back from the desk so that her whole body is turned towards Joe. She sits in an upright but relaxed position, with her limbs uncrossed, and inclines towards him just slightly, making full eye contact. Helen's non-verbal signals indicate that she is ready to listen sympathetically, and her posture and facial expressions, as well as her words, encourage Joe to say what is worrying him.

ACTIVITY 41: *Responding to deception*

(a) Choose three occasions when someone's body language might make you think that the person was not being entirely truthful. (You could choose some of the situations that you identified in Activity 38 or focus on something that you may have to deal with in the future.)

(b) Decide what outcome you want. For example, do you want to make the person admit the lie, or at least give a more honest and accurate answer? You might want to develop the discussion, or to encourage the person to say more. The outcome you want will shape your verbal and non-verbal communication.

(c) Think about the body language that will be appropriate for you to use.

Situation	Desired outcome	Body language
1		
2		
3		

Hiding your emotions

There will be occasions at work when you want to disguise your real feelings. You may not want anyone to know that you are feeling sad, for example, or disappointed, or that you are very worried about something. However, it is very likely that a close observer will pick up micro-signals in you – such as a downturned mouth and trembling lips.

Scene 25: Crispin hides his disappointment

Crispin has just been told that he has not received the promotion that he had expected. He feels very disappointed and angry, but manages to control his expression and gestures. Back at his desk, he is aware that his eyes are smarting, and he can feel his mouth trembling.

Crispin needs a little time alone. He indicates that he does not want to talk to anyone by looking down at his desk with his hands on either side of his face, and spreads his elbows so that they create a physical barrier. This gives the signal that he is concentrating and does not want to be disturbed. He reinforces this impression by surrounding himself with piles of books and papers.

In this way, Crispin uses his body language to keep others away until he feels that he can interact with them without revealing his disappointed feelings.

How to Read Body Language More Accurately

Why we sometimes get it wrong

It is important to be accurate in our interpretation of others' non-verbal signals – but it is not always easy. Even though you are aware of the significance of clusters of signs, and take into account the context in which the communication takes place, there are a number of factors that can distort your perception. We all view the world through our own filters, made up of all the things that make us unique, and through which every external stimulus passes before we perceive it. We all see things differently, as our judgements and responses are influenced by our past experiences and our expectations. It is very easy to be swayed by biases and prejudices that we are hardly aware we have. This distortion can take place in a variety of ways and for a variety of reasons.

The halo effect

We want to have a coherent picture of someone, so we judge a person on the basis of one or two characteristics, which may be positive or negative. We attribute someone with a range of qualities that they may or may not possess.

For example, Nessa sees that her new supervisor, Joyce, walks in a very confident manner. Her stride seems purposeful and energetic. Nessa thinks that Joyce will be good at her job and that she will make quick decisions, and she has the impression that Joyce will keep strict deadlines. Nessa is demonstrating the power of what is called the 'halo effect'. Her perception of Joyce's abilities is based purely on one observable characteristic.

Seeing what we expect to see

Our interpretation of people's behaviour can be strongly influenced by expectations that have been set up. If you are told that someone has a great sense of humour, you will be tuned into every example of behaviour that illustrates this. If you are told that the same person has no sense of humour, you will be ready to have this judgement confirmed.

Peter has a reputation of being something of a flirt. When Anna is allocated to work in his section she comments to her friends that he held her gaze for rather too long, and sat too close to her when he was showing her how to use the switchboard. It is possible that Anna's judgement and interpretation of Peter's behaviour is influenced by what she has heard.

Seeing what we need to see

Our own needs affect the way that we perceive the world around us. If you are thinking of buying a new car, you will see signs and advertisements that you may not particularly notice at another time. Suddenly the roads are full of the kind of car that you have in mind. You may have noticed that when you are hungry, the sight and smell of food seem to be everywhere. Once you have eaten, you are far less aware of this stimulus.

Lena has a strong need for social interaction at work. It is very important to her to have friendly relationships with her co-workers. She thinks that her boss, Samir, is aloof and unfriendly. Rebecca's social needs are not as developed as Lena's, and she finds that Samir's manner is pleasant and professional.

Wanting to make it fit

We ignore or distort any information that conflicts with the first impression or a fixed impression that we have developed of someone.

The first time that Denise sees Mark she decides that he is pushy and confrontational. She watches him in conversation with a colleague.

Mark is standing with his feet wide apart and his arms folded, and seems to be aggressive and impatient (Figure 12).

As their working relationship develops, Mark shows that he is willing to negotiate and discuss matters. He does like to exert his authority, but tries not to behave aggressively. However,

Figure 12 *An aggressive stance*

Denise does not take in these messages. Her first impression of Mark is fixed in her mind, and she is hanging on to it.

Stereotyping

We may apply stereotyping, and make assumptions about people based on one or two characteristics that they share with particular groups. This is what happens when we think of all the members of a group of people as being identical. For example, we might label people according to certain aspects of their appearance. We may make assumptions about blonde women, or men with moustaches, or about people who wear certain items of dress or jewellery.

How to get it right

Don't make hasty judgements

We can build on our observation of others' body language, rather than be misled by it, if we stop ourselves from making judgements too quickly. Of course, we are strongly influenced by first impressions, but we have to avoid our whole evaluation of a person on the basis of the signals that we pick up at a first meeting.

Be ready to adapt your first assessment, if necessary, as you process more information about a person.

See things from the other person's point of view

Put yourself in the other person's shoes. Try to step outside your own frame of reference and see the situation from their point of view. Seeing things from another's perspective will help you to make balanced assessments of their non-verbal communication.

Listen to what people say

The more you understand someone's thoughts and emotions, the more likely you are to interpret their body language accurately. Actively listening to someone is the key to greater communication and understanding. Chapter 6 discusses how your understanding of body language can help you to become a more effective listener in a number of work situations.

ACTIVITY 42: Picking up all the cues

Just as you may be in the habit of using certain gestures and facial expressions, so you may be in the habit of responding to certain aspects of body language, and not seeing the others.

Choose one or two people whose non-verbal communication you regularly observe. Make a note in each column about what you see. For any aspect that you find difficult to comment on because you have not observed it sufficiently, make a point of concentrating on that aspect of the person's body language over the next week or two.

	Person a	*Person b*
Dress		
Appearance		
Way of standing		
Way of walking		
Way of sitting		
Use of space		
Facial expression		
Head movements		
Hand movements		

6

Building Rapport

It is more than likely that you have mixed feelings about your co-workers. There will be some with whom you get on well, and you might say that you have particular rapport with these individuals. By this you mean that you share a feeling of being connected to and in harmony with one another, and that you have bonded as colleagues – and possibly even as friends. No doubt there are other people at work with whom you would say that you have no rapport whatsoever, and it is probably true to say that you cannot imagine yourself ever feeling in sympathy with this other person or people. However, if you wish to, you can develop good relationships, and even rapport, with people with whom you feel no affinity and with whom you have no natural bond. You can improve the quality of your working relationships and reach more satisfactory outcomes in a whole range of situations through applying some comparatively recent ideas that link the way that we think with the way that we communicate verbally and non-verbally. By recognizing your own patterns, and

tuning into other people's, you can overcome some of the barriers to communication and build a relationship of trust and confidence. As with all aspects of communication, there are two concepts that are central to the successful building of relationships:

- **Respect for the other**
  You have to be able to accept other people's points of view and the way in which they communicate, which may of course be very different from your own.
- **Personal congruence**
  Your own values and beliefs are at the core of your being, and are revealed in all aspects of your behaviour. If you try to be someone you are not, your true beliefs will leak out.

Different Minds, Different Patterns

In the 1970s Richard Bandler and John Grinder created a system of techniques and skills that would enable people to become more successful in their business and personal relationships through applying certain psychological tools.

They called this process Neuro-Linguistic Programming (NLP). There are some skilled communicators who use the principles of this system without realizing it – and these are the people who seem to get on with everyone and to be well liked, the people who seem to be successful in their business relationships and outcomes. This success may well be based on their ability to pick up cues from others' verbal and non-verbal language, and to adjust their own behaviour accordingly.

NLP offers a structure for understanding certain aspects of the way in which we communicate:

- Neuro: the way that we use our brain and all of our senses – seeing, hearing, touching, smelling and tasting.
- Linguistic: the way that we use language to communicate.
- Programming: our repeated patterns of thinking and behaving.

Tune Into Your Own System

We experience our world through the five senses. We process the information that we absorb in mental pictures, or sounds, or smells, or tastes, or feelings. Some people 'see' something, while others 'feel' it. Some of us 'hear' it. We all have our own preferred way of using our senses. Probably at various times we use them all, but it is likely that we have one that dominates our perception. Knowing your own mode of perception will increase your awareness of the way in which you communicate. When you are aware of the way that the people with whom you work process *their* experience, you can tune into their wavelength and build rapport with them. Realizing how other people use their senses can help you to understand their behaviour and lead to more effective communication.

The terms used to describe the senses are:

- Visual: thinking in pictures.
- Auditory: thinking in sounds.
- Kinaesthetic: thinking in feelings.

Taste and smell, the other senses, are less frequently and consistently used in Western society, although phrases such as 'Wake up and smell the coffee' and 'It's so close I can taste it' are a familiar part of our language.

Three areas of behaviour can give us an overview of how people think:

- Eye movements.
- Choice of words.
- Body language.

We can develop rapport with others, and build relationships based on respect and understanding, through recognizing and responding to the cues that we pick up from these aspects of behaviour.

Eye Movements and Thinking Styles

The direction in which our eyes move when we are thinking can give some indication of which system we prefer.

ACTIVITY 43: Eye directions

As you think about each of the following, observe in which direction your eyes move. Notice, for example, when they move up and to the right, and when they move down and to the left. Describe or draw your eye movements for each suggestion. If you prefer, you could ask someone else to do the exercise while you observe how their eyes move.

Bring to mind   *Eye movements*

(a) How many windows there are in your home _____

(b) What your boss would look like in a clown's outfit _____

(c) What someone at work said to you yesterday _____

(d) Your boss speaking to you in a baby voice _____

(e) A time when you felt very sad _____

(f) What you say to yourself when you are
getting psyched up for something _____

(g) The face of someone you love _____

It is likely that (if you are right-handed) your eyes moved in the following ways. If you are left-handed, some of the sideways movements may be reversed.

(a) Up and to the left. This is usually what our eyes do when we visualize something from our past experience.

(b) Up and to the right. This is usually what our eyes do when we visualize something we are constructing or imagining.

(c) Sideways and to the left. This is usually what our eyes do when we remember sounds.

(d) Sideways and to the right. This is usually what our eyes do when we are constructing or imagining sounds.

(e) Down and to the right. This is usually what our eyes do when we are accessing feelings.

(f) Down and to the left. This is usually what our eyes do when we are engaging in dialogue with ourselves.

(g) Straight ahead. This is usually what our eyes do when we are visualizing and concentrating on a picture in our head.

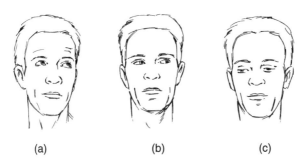

Figure 13 *Eye movements*

ACTIVITY 44: Cue the eyes

Based on what you have learnt in Activity 43, match up the eye movements in Figure 13 and the following thoughts:

1 Last year's holiday _____

2 The tune of a song _____

3 A tense situation _____

Answers: 1(a); 2(b); 3(c).

Watching someone's eye movements during your conversations and interactions is a step towards finding out if the person thinks in pictures, sounds or feelings. As a general rule, a visual thinker's eyes move to the right, an auditory thinker's eyes move to the left, and the eyes of a kinaesthetic thinker look down.

Scene 26: Maria tunes into Justin's way of thinking

Maria wants to build a good working relationship with Justin, who has recently become her manager. She hopes that he will like some of the ideas that she wants to put into practice. One of the ways in which Maria tries to tune into Justin's way of thinking is by watching his eye movements. She notices that when they are discussing work matters, Justin's eyes move up to the right. This makes her think that Justin may be a predominantly visual thinker – one who sees pictures in his head. Maria needs to check out her observation by paying attention to other aspects of Justin's verbal and non-verbal behaviour, but if her observation is accurate, she may be able to build on her understanding of how Justin's mind works, and to generate rapport in their professional relationship.

ACTIVITY 45: Verbal patterns

Put the following phrases into one of the three main categories. Put a tick in the box under the appropriate heading:

	Visual	Auditory	Kinaesthetic
1 Getting a perspective	☐	☐	☐
2 Getting a grip	☐	☐	☐
3 Singing from the same sheet	☐	☐	☐
4 Loud and clear	☐	☐	☐
5 Getting bogged down	☐	☐	☐
6 Boiling point	☐	☐	☐
7 A clear picture	☐	☐	☐
8 A smooth ride	☐	☐	☐
9 Seeing eye to eye	☐	☐	☐
10 Gut feeling	☐	☐	☐
11 We need to discuss	☐	☐	☐
12 We need to explore	☐	☐	
13 Face the situation	☐	☐	☐
14 Teething problems	☐	☐	☐
15 Gets under my skin	☐	☐	☐

Answers: 1, 7, 9 and 13 are visual; 3, 4 and 11 are auditory; 2, 5, 6, 8, 10, 12, 14 and 15 are kinaesthetic.

This Activity reflects how much we tend to use each style. More of us think in the kinaesthetic mode (feelings) than in other modes. The next most common style is the visual, followed by the auditory system.

Patterns of Words

Your eye movements give a clue as to whether you think mainly in pictures, or in sounds, or in feelings. Your preference may also be reflected in the words that you use. If your thinking is predominantly visual, you are likely to use language such as 'I see what you mean' or 'That looks fine to me'. An auditory thinker may use expressions such as 'That sounds the right thing to do' or 'If I'm hearing you correctly...', whereas a kinaesthetic thinker may talk about a 'gut feeling' or 'getting in touch'.

Activity 46 will help you to become aware of the kinds of phrases that individuals use.

ACTIVITY 46: Tune into words

Choose three people with whom you work and listen to the kind of words and phrases that they use. Jot these down and put them into the appropriate category:

	Feeling phrases	*Seeing phrases*	*Hearing phrases*
Person a			
Person b			
Person c			

Mind and Body

Our thinking processes can also be reflected in our non-verbal communication. The way we walk and stand, the gestures that we use, the way we breathe, and the sound of our voice may indicate our preferred way of processing information.

Visual thinkers

People who think visually tend to speak quickly in a high-pitched tone. Their posture is straight and upright, a little tense around the shoulders, and their breathing is shallow, centred in the upper part of the chest. Sometimes they have faint lines across the forehead, even if the rest of the face is smooth, as a result of raising the brow when thinking of something.

Auditory thinkers

Those who access information in terms of sounds speak in clear, resonant, melodic tones. Their breath is evenly paced over the full chest range, and their posture is well balanced, with the head sometimes inclined to one side, as if listening.

Kinaesthetic thinkers

People who represent information in terms of feelings speak in deep, slow tones, taking their time to describe how they feel. They breathe deep down in their abdomen, and their posture is relaxed, with the head pointing downwards.

ACTIVITY 47: Do you hear, see or feel things?

Imagine that you are giving someone instructions about how to do something. It could be how to use a function on a computer (you might choose to use words like 'drag' and 'pull'), or how to cook a certain dish, or it could be directions about how to get somewhere. How do you go about it? What kinds of words and phrases do you use? What kind of body language do you use? If you like, you could ask a friend to observe you giving the instructions and to provide you with feedback to help you fill in the chart below:

	Examples	Is this the visual, auditory or kinaesthetic mode?
Words		
Posture		
Tone of voice		
Gestures		

ACTIVITY 48: Try other systems

These exercises will help you to develop insight into different ways of thinking, and to move more flexibly through different sensory systems.

A

Describe what method you would use to memorize each of the following examples, and write the initial letter of the word to indicate if your method is visual, auditory or kinaesthetic. The first example has been done for you:

Example	Method	V / A / K
A shopping list	Repeat the items out loud	A

(a) The route of a journey from
your home to an airport _____

(b) Your computer password _____

(c) The names of three
new people at work _____

Now choose a different mode of thought to remember the examples. As well as your own ideas, you could choose from the following: writing; drawing; visualizing; making up rhymes; making funny pictures in your head; making links; putting yourself in the situation; creating a story; using images and symbols; making emotional associations.

Example	Method	V / A / K
A shopping list	Picturing the items	V

(a) The route of a journey from
your home to an airport _____

(b) Your computer password _____

(c) The names of three
new people at work _____

B

Experiment by concentrating on each sense in turn. Spend one day in visual mode, one when you are dominantly auditory, and one when you experience through your senses. For each day, decide on specific actions. For example, on your visual day you could focus on the range of different colours that you see during the day, and on your auditory day you could monitor all the different sounds that you hear in certain places at certain times.

	Visual day	*Auditory day*	*Kinaesthetic day*
Action 1			
Action 2			
Action 3			
Action 4			
Action 5			
Action 6			

Signs of Rapport

Think about the friends and colleagues who you like and with whom you get on well. It is probable that you are alike in some ways. You may share the same tastes, or have similar life experiences. It is likely that you have good relationships with those who have the same values as you, and who view the world in the same way. You may well enjoy the company of people who have the same kinds of skills and abilities as you. The early stages of friendship are often spent finding out what you have in common and establishing common ground.

When a friendship or close connection is established, you might have noticed that people often speak in the same way as each other, and even have the same kinds of mannerisms. When they talk they assume similar postures, both sitting with crossed legs or folded arms, for example (Figure 14).

People who share the rapport of friendship seem to be in harmony with each other, communicating in the same way and with the same pace and rhythm. When you are having a drink or a meal with a friend, it is likely that your movements and the gaps between eating and

83

drinking and talking are synchronized. This occurs spontaneously, as a result of the relationship. Such behaviour also helps to maintain and develop the feeling of closeness and rapport, because of our natural tendency to like people who are similar to us.

Figure 14 *Mirroring posture*

Match and Mirror

You can use the technique of matching, or mirroring as it is also called, by tuning into someone's way of thinking and body language, and using the same kind of language and actions yourself. This is a way of building rapport and communication, as the other person unconsciously feels a sense of connection with you, and by experiencing the other person's world

ACTIVITY 49: Matching behaviours

Choose a pair of close friends to observe, at work or at home. If you prefer, you could watch a scene on television or video that depicts a conversation between two people who are good friends. Note any examples of matching behaviour in the chart below. Notice echoes and similarities, not necessarily identical examples.

	Person a	Person b
Words/phrases		
Tone of voice		
Pace of speaking		
Posture		
Gestures		
Body movement		
Facial expression		

you unconsciously enter into it and achieve a higher level of understanding of the way they think and feel.

It is important to realize that this is not an exercise in mimicry. If you mechanically copy someone's behaviour you will damage communication, not strengthen it. Matching is a sign of acknowledgement and recognition of the other person and indicates a desire for understanding and enhanced communication. You may be sensitive to someone's standpoint, but if you mismatch signals, your behaviour might not demonstrate your sensitivity.

Mirroring posture

Adopting the same posture as someone enables you to build rapport. We have already seen how you can use physical movements to help you to create feelings and moods. Matching someone's body movements is a way of entering into that

85

person's frame of mind. For example, if someone is feeling down and depressed, this may be reflected in slumped posture. Try adopting that posture yourself. You will find it difficult to maintain an upbeat attitude while your body is experiencing very different feelings, and you will gain understanding of the other person.

Scene 27: Maria matches Justin's body style

Maria's observations of Justin's choice of words and his body movements confirm her feeling that Justin is a visual thinker. She tunes into his wavelength and tries to see the world as he sees it. Maria herself does not prefer the visual mode, but she 'tries it on' to get in touch with Justin's way of seeing the world. She sits in the same way as Justin, straight and upright, with her eyes turned up, and finds that this helps her to think visually. In this position, she will be able to access the kind of visual language that Justin uses.

Justin tends to sit well back in his chair with his head pointed towards the ceiling. When he is very interested in what is being said he leans forward and makes a sweeping gesture with his palms up. Maria mirrors his behaviour, leaning forward when he does, and making a modified version of the same gesture.

Matching the words

Using the same kind of language as someone is an effective way of establishing and developing rapport. You could pick up some of the words that someone uses and feed them into your own speech, and you could choose other words and phrases from the same system. When you are speaking to a kinaesthetic person, use words that have a sensory appeal and that relate to feelings. If you are communicating with a visual thinker, use language that creates pictures to refer to your point of view. With an auditory thinker use words to do with sounds, and speak as fluently and clearly as you can.

Sharing someone's preferred style shows awareness and sensitivity, and indicates your desire to establish common ground.

Activity 51 will give you some ideas about different categories of language.

Scene 28: Maria matches Justin's language

Maria uses the same kinds of phrases as Justin. She says to him, 'I see what you mean' and 'I think we will get a clearer picture if we . . .' Justin's nods, his facial expressions and his eye contact show that he is responding positively to what she is saying.

When Maria wants to demonstrate or illustrate a point to Justin she uses visual means. She supports her words by sketching out a chart or diagram, or writing down key words for him to see.

Voice matching

Think of somebody who talks much more quickly or much more slowly than you do. It is more than likely that when you are with this person you unconsciously adapt the rate at which you speak. This does not mean that you speak at exactly the same pace, but that to a

ACTIVITY 50: Mirroring language

Think of someone at work with whom you would like to communicate more effectively. Listen to the words and phrases that this person uses, and choose some examples of similar language that you can use in your next encounter.

Words and phrases the person uses   *Words and phrases I will use*

1 _____

2 _____

3 _____

4 _____

5 _____

6 _____

certain extent you speed up or slow down. You can develop this natural instinct in order to bring about enhanced communication by speaking at the same pace and in the same tone of voice as the other person.

We all speak in certain intonations and rhythms that are characteristic of our individual ways of talking. You may be able to think of someone who speaks in a monotone with little variation in the tone of voice. You may know someone whose voice has a singsong rhythm, or someone who speaks in short bursts. Adapting your own style so that it mirrors the other

person's can be done quite imperceptibly, and will create a sense of rapport between you.

Matching breathing

Breathing in the same way as the person to whom you are speaking emphasizes the fact that you are paying attention and makes the other person feel relaxed. To help you to tune into someone's breathing pattern, just remember that we breathe out when we speak, and we take in a breath when we pause or stop speaking. The rise and fall of the chest area and of the shoulders also indicate our rate of breathing. You may need to practise a bit, particularly if you are communicating with someone whose breathing is markedly different from yours.

Scene 29: Maria mirrors Justin's voice and breathing

Maria observes that Justin, a visual thinker, speaks at a fairly high pitch and breathes and speaks quickly. It is almost as if the words are tumbling out to keep up with the pictures in his mind. Maria imagines that her voice is coming from up inside her head. She can feel the pitch of her voice rise, and she finds that she can match the tone and rhythm of his speech.

Maria's observation of Justin's behaviour and her ability to match it unobtrusively leads to the creation of rapport. This does not mean that Justin agrees with everything that Maria says, but communication flows easily, attention is engaged, and they are occupying common ground. Maria's sensitive and skilful response to Justin's style means that he knows that she is working with him. Mutual understanding is established, and their professional relationship is enjoyable and productive.

ACTIVITY 51: Voice matching

Focus on the person you chose for Activity 50. Observe how he or she talks and breathes, and practise mirroring it. Put a tick in the 'Matched' box when you have mirrored this quality in communication. What is the effect of this quality? Try this technique in your next conversation with the person.

	Description	Matched	Effect
Tone of voice	_____	☐	_____
Pace of speaking	_____	☐	_____
Pitch of voice	_____	☐	_____
Volume of voice	_____	☐	_____
Rhythm of speech	_____	☐	_____
Pace of breathing	_____	☐	_____

Pacing and leading

Once you are tuned into someone's emotional state and can match it in your own behaviour, you are in a position to change someone's mood. You do this by meeting their mood with your non-verbal signals, then changing your behaviour slightly to lead the person in the direction you would like them to move. This technique can work very well if you are trying to calm down an angry customer or co-worker (see Chapter 7), and can also be a way of generating enthusiasm or encouraging agreement.

Scene 30: Petra negotiates for a four-day week

Petra would like to change her working week to four days instead of five. She has prepared some convincing arguments for her case, but knows that the initial reaction of Sheryll, her boss, will be to say no.

When Petra goes to talk to Sheryll about it, she does not begin at a high pitch of persuasion. Sheryll is sitting with her arms and legs crossed, and listens with a slight frown. Her voice is not enthusiastic. Petra assumes a similar posture, and maintains a serious expression, matching Sheryll's frown. She speaks in the same kind of tone as Sheryll – level and even rather than excited or persuasive.

As the conversation continues, Petra shifts into more open body language, and raises her voice slightly. She notices that Sheryll's posture and gestures change, and that her

voice is more lively and engaged. Whether Petra gets what she wants or not, she has led Sheryll past the closed, automatic refusal state to a position of more interest, from which they can negotiate productively.

Taking things step by step

This technique is unlikely to be effective if you mismatch signals, or try to lead someone too quickly. It is important to establish rapport before you move on.

Scene 31: Amelia is agitated

Amelia knocks on the head of year's door. 'Can I talk to you about that bullying yesterday?' she says.

'Come in and sit down,' says Lesley. She notices that Amelia seems agitated. She is breathing rapidly and twisting her hands together, and when she starts to explain what happened, her voice is shrill and shaky.

Lesley feels very sympathetic towards Amelia's nervous state, but wants her to calm down so that they can discuss the matter. She speaks to Amelia in a low calm voice, and sits in a relaxed position with her hands open, hoping that Amelia will respond to these cues and behave in a less agitated way. Lesley is very surprised when Amelia gets up and goes to the door.

'I knew you wouldn't understand,' she says. I knew it would be a waste of time trying to talk to you.'

Lesley is baffled. She had been listening sympathetically to Amelia, and wanted to help. She knew that her verbal and non-verbal responses had not been threatening or off-putting, so what could have gone wrong?

Lesley's body language did not reflect the sympathy that she felt. In her desire to help Amelia to calm down, she modelled calm behaviour too quickly, without first establishing rapport through matching Amelia's behaviour.

ACTIVITY 52: How it could have been done (see Scene 31)

What body language could Lesley have used when Amelia started to speak? _____

_____

What posture could she have used? _____

_____

What gestures could she have made? _____

_____

How could she have spoken? _____

_____

Communication Clashes

Scene 32: Ryan upsets Stella

Ryan is very pleased with Stella's contribution to the open day. At the end, he goes round the whole team and shakes hands with each one, saying, 'Thanks a lot for all you did to make this such a success.' He gives Stella a particularly warm handclasp and further conveys his acknowledgement of her excellent work with a sincere smile and sustained eye contact.

'All he did was say thank you,' Stella grumbles afterwards. And he said that to everyone. I had to do much more work than the others, and I think I made a good job of it. It would be nice to have it acknowledged. I won't bother next time.'

Ryan's dominant mode of behaviour is kinaesthetic. He is tuned into touch and feelings, and has expressed his thanks and gratitude for Stella's work in the way that is natural to him. Stella, however, is dominantly auditory. She needs to hear the words spoken;

ACTIVITY 53: Pacing and leading

Think of an occasion when you might want to change someone's mood – to get them to cheer up, for example, or to become more serious about what you are discussing. Choose someone whose behaviour you know well, so that you can plan your own actions.

Person: _____

Mood or emotional state: _____

Aspects of body language that show this:

Posture	Gestures	Voice	Facial expressions

Body language I will use/avoid:

Posture	Gestures	Voice	Facial expressions

Desired mood or emotional state: _____

How I will lead with my body language:

Posture	Gestures	Voice	Facial expressions

she likes to remember and repeat any positive comments that she receives. Stella cannot recall the feel of Ryan's handclasp and the impact of his gaze because she was hardly aware of them. She was waiting to hear what he was going to say to her.

In cases such as this, the situation will be improved only if one of the people involved recognizes the differences between them, and is willing to adjust his or her own style.

Scene 33: Sean changes his channel of communication

Sean manages a regional branch of a finance company, and has to keep in regular contact with Alan at the head office. They exchange e-mails frequently, and although the relevant information is exchanged, there are some requests or questions to which Alan does not seem to respond very quickly, and Sean often has to send a reminder.

When Sean meets Alan face to face he observes his eye movements, and the way that he talks and moves. Sean thinks that Alan might prefer to process information in an auditory way. Sean tries telephoning Alan instead of communicating by e-mail, and finds that he rarely has to chase anything up, and the quality of their communication is greatly improved.

ACTIVITY 54: Matching different types

For each of the following situations, think of what you could say using each of the three systems:

1 Being unable to meet a work deadline

Statement in hearing mode: _____

_____

Statement in seeing mode: _____

_____

Statement in feeling mode: _____

_____

2 Asking for time off

Statement in hearing mode: _____

_____

Statement in seeing mode: _____

_____

Statement in feeling mode: _____

_____

3 Proposing a change in an established work practice

Statement in hearing mode: _____

_____

Statement in seeing mode: _____

_____

Statement in feeling mode: _____

_____

7

Testing Situations

Meetings

Before the meeting

Before any work-related meeting, do some thinking about:

- Your role in the meeting.
- The outcome that you want.
- The other participants – their positions and interests.

The reason and purpose for your attendance at a meeting will vary according to the situation. Your objective may be to sell an idea, or to challenge someone else's suggestions. You may wish solely to make a good impression on another participant, perhaps your boss, or someone else you wish to impress. Your main objective may be to escape at the end without being asked to contribute or having anyone notice your presence. Perhaps you regard certain meetings as arenas in which you can flex your competitive muscles, wind people up or have some fun. We all use meetings to fulfil needs other than those that are stated as the meeting's

objectives. For some people, their need to feel part of a cohesive group will determine the way they behave. These participants relate to the social and personal aspects of the meeting. Others, who need to achieve and get things done, will focus on getting through the agenda quickly and effectively. There will be other people whose need to display power shapes their behaviour and responses.

Once you are clear about the way that you need to present yourself at the meeting, you can think about how to project appropriate non-verbal signals. Identifying others' needs and agendas will enable you to tap into their motivations to bring the meeting to a satisfying outcome.

Scene 34: The department meeting (1)

Ravi knows that he is going to have to handle the department meeting very carefully. He is chairing the meeting, and the main item on the agenda is his proposal for changing the present system of reporting on students' progress. Ravi is anticipating some opposition to

ACTIVITY 55: Different agendas

Think about a meeting you have recently attended or, if you prefer, focus on one due to take place soon. Describe your business objectives for the meeting, and your personal objectives. Do the same for two other participants.

	Meeting	Business objectives	Personal objectives
Myself			
Person a			
Person b			

his idea, although he is not sure exactly who will support him and who will oppose.

Lorraine is anxious about the meeting. She wants to listen to what Ravi has to say, and she has some points that she really wants to make, but she sometimes finds it difficult to get a word in edgeways.

Paul is going to speak against Ravi's proposal. He wants to give forceful objections to it, and to persuade others to agree with him.

Michelle thinks Ravi's idea is a good one. She doesn't always agree with him, but in this case she wants to show her support.

How to arrive

It is important to arrive on time. Whether you are in charge of the meeting or a participant, arriving late gives the impression that the meeting and the people involved are a low priority for you. Walking into the room with a bright welcoming

95

facial expression and energetic movements indicates that you will be a positive presence at the meeting, and your positive impression may well have an energizing influence on the mood of the other participants.

If you are unavoidably delayed, take a moment outside the door to get yourself into a calm, unflustered state of mind. Make sure that your posture is upright. Enter the room quietly, with a brief word or nod of apology, or reason if you think it is necessary, and take your seat unobtrusively. You should not make exaggerated 'I'm trying to be quiet and not be noticed' movements, nor should you make a disturbance when arranging your chair or depositing items on the table.

The materials that you take with you to a meeting convey messages about your attitude. You will create an impression of being prepared and professional if you carry any documents relevant to the meeting, and a writing pad or notebook. A newspaper folded to display the crossword, or papers and work unrelated to the meeting, indicate that you will not be giving it your full attention.

Scene 34: The department meeting (2)

Ravi is in the meeting room five minutes before the start time, ready to greet people as they arrive. Lorraine and Michelle come in together, each carrying a copy of the agenda and the related documents. Anthea bustles in with a set of student assignments in her hand and a preoccupied frown on her face. Phil, who is in charge of charity events, enters

smiling cheerily at everyone and jangling a tin of coins. Paul is the last to arrive.

In this situation, the way that Anthea takes work into the meeting not only gives the impression that her mind will be elsewhere, but suggests that she thinks her time would be better spent grading student essays. Some may also feel that she is showing them how hard she works. Phil's mode of entry could indicate that the meeting is an intrusion into more important business, although his smile suggests a co-operative attitude. One or two of the participants, Ravi in particular, eye the tin of coins and hope that Phil is not intending to count them during the meeting.

Where to sit

The places in which people sit are important in two ways. First, the nature of the communication is affected by the seating arrangements and the space and distance between people. Second, by choosing a certain seat or place, you communicate something about your attitude. Research into proxemics (see page 44) shows that seating arrangements influence our perception of interpersonal relationships. Our choice of whether to sit opposite someone, or side by side, or at an angle, and the distances at which we sit, give a message about our relationship with the person and the nature of the meeting.

Sitting face to face can suggest unfriendliness or the expectation of a competitive or hostile encounter. By choosing such a position you indicate something of an adversarial approach. In addition, the positioning itself can create such an atmosphere, encouraging each person to take up a competitive or defensive stance. Our territorial instincts come into play, and we each lay claim to the half of the table that divides us. This is not a position that is conducive to discussion or negotiation – it is too likely to lead to antagonism.

Sitting side by side can indicate a spirit of support and co-operation; it can also create an atmosphere of trust and support. By sitting at someone's side, you are seen to be – and indeed can feel that you are – on that person's side with regard to the matters under discussion.

Corner diagonal positions are associated with friendly informality. Such a position, with the corner of the table providing a slight barrier and prop, is a compromise between the across-the-table and side-by-side stances.

The most powerful position at a meeting table is either in the middle of one of the long sides, particularly the one facing the door, or at the short end of the table. This position indicates a leadership role. The person occupying it has visual control of the meeting, and the importance of other participants is defined by their distance from the leader. Those closest to the authority figure are seen to be those most in favour.

A round meeting table tends to present fewer issues of power and status, as the shape of the table symbolizes equality and democracy. However, it is still the case that wherever the most powerful person sits, those on either side of them are seen to be the next in the pecking order.

ACTIVITY 56: Seating arrangements

Think about the last meeting you attended. On a piece of paper, draw a diagram of the table or meeting space. Write the name of the participants, including yourself, in the places people chose to sit:

Why did you choose your particular position? If you in fact had no choice regarding where you sat, where would you have chosen to sit? Why?

_____

_____

How far did people's preferred seating positions reflect the relationships within the group?

_____

_____

During the meeting

How you sit

The way that you sit on your chair and position your body gives non-verbal messages that may support your verbal contribution, or contradict it. If you are at a table, only the upper half of your body can be seen, so your posture, hand, head and eye movements are important. Sitting straight in your chair indicates alertness and involvement, and generates a feeling of warmth from others. However, if you sit bolt upright on the edge of your seat you may seem strained and tense. A relaxed upright posture communicates interest and commitment to the meeting. Slouching or leaning right back in a casual pose often indicates indifference and rejection, and says that you are not interested in the proceedings. Sometimes, however, leaning back in your chair may be appropriate if the atmosphere of the meeting is informal, but remember that this posture may indicate a superior attitude, especially if your hands are clasped behind your neck, and could irritate the others present. A much more positive impression is created if you prop up your head on one hand between the thumb and first two fingers. This will usually be interpreted as a sign that you are listening and taking an intelligent interest. Be careful not to let your eyelids droop, though, as this will be seen as boredom. Cocking your head at a bit of an angle also indicates that you are paying attention. Charles Darwin noted that animals as well as humans tilt their heads when they are interested in something. (It has been observed that this gesture is more commonly used by women than men, and that it is often seen as being a flirtatious signal.)

It is not a good idea to fold your arms. Folded arms will often be interpreted as defensive, especially if the rest of your verbal and non-verbal assertions indicate that you want to protect yourself from what is going on. This posture may also be seen as an aggressive pose, especially if accompanied by a glaring expression. However, if your arms are folded on the desk, but your body is leaning forward and your expression is open and interested, the position of your arms may just indicate that you are comfortable sitting like that. Generally, the *orientation* of your body

Figure 15 *Feet pointing away from conversation*

– that is, its angle and the direction in which it points – is said to indicate the direction of your real feelings. If your body, or parts of it, points away from the person who is speaking or to whom you are speaking, you could be perceived as having a negative attitude towards that person (Figure 15). This impression may be reinforced or contradicted by the words that you speak.

Scene 34: The department meeting (3)

Ravi takes the seat at the top end of the oblong table. He establishes his territory by placing the meeting materials in front of him and sitting with his arms spread open on the arms of his chair. Ravi notices that Michelle sits next to him, and gives him a friendly nod as she takes her seat. Lorraine sits next to Michelle and smiles in greeting. Ravi is relieved to see that Phil puts his tin of coins under the table, but his relief is short-lived when Phil takes out his cellphone and cradles it in his hand. Anthea places her pile of work in front of her, forming a barrier between herself and the rest of the meeting. Paul arrives just as the meeting is about to begin and sits opposite Ravi at the other end of the table. He looks as if he means business. He is upright and relaxed in his chair, leaning forward with his hands placed on the table as if he is ready to speak. Even before the meeting has begun, Ravi has the impression that Michelle will support his proposal and Paul will oppose it. He is not sure about Lorraine. He feels that Anthea and Phil will not be giving the meeting their full attention, whatever they may feel about the proposal under discussion.

How you behave

Your non-verbal behaviour throughout a meeting can create a strong impression, either negative or positive, and can help or hinder you in achieving the outcome you want. You will be seen as attentive and responsive if you look at each person who speaks, and respond visually with gestures such as nodding and raising your eyebrows slightly. Even if you do not say very much at a meeting, you can communicate your interest and create a positive impression by giving active non-verbal responses to what is going on.

When you speak, try not to address your remarks to one person only. It is very easy to look just at the person chairing the meeting, or at the person to whom you are responding, but if you do this your comments will have less impact on the rest of the meeting. Instead, look at everyone as you speak. You may not be able to make eye contact with each individual, but do include everyone in your glance.

Control the movements of your hands and your head. An emphatic hand gesture to reinforce what you are saying will add strength to your contribution, but flapping hand movements will make you seem less confident and will distract people from what you are actually saying. Keep your hands away from your face and your mouth while you are speaking. Touching your nose or your mouth as you talk may be seen as a suggestion that you are not telling the truth or that you are insincere, and in any case is likely to make your words less distinct.

Make head movements to emphasize what you say. Stress the importance of certain words or phrases with little downward movements of your head – but be careful not to overdo this. It is more natural for us to nod frequently when we are listening than when we are speaking.

99

Scene 34: The department meeting (4)

As Ravi presents his proposal he watches how people behave. Michelle's body and head are turned towards him, and out of the corner of his eye he can see her nodding in agreement with certain statements. Paul listens intently with his chin propped against his thumb (Figure 16). His other fingers are below his mouth. His body is drawn back and turned slightly away from Ravi. This cluster of gestures indicates that Paul is critical of what he is hearing. However, his head is not being supported by his hand, which is an encouraging sign for Ravi. In general, the level of criticism is signalled by how heavily the head is leaning on the hand.

Phil has his head tilted at an angle as if he is listening, but he reveals his impatience to be off and sorting out his tin of money in the way that he drums his fingers on the table. Anthea does not look up from her marking. Lorraine is leaning forward with her head turned towards Ravi and her hand on her cheek, indicating her interest in what he is saying. Her index finger points up, suggesting that she is evaluating what Ravi says (Figure 17).

Ravi comes to the end of his talk. The gestures of the others at this point show that they are making up their minds about what he has said. Lorraine has her hands clasped beneath her chin with her index fingers in the steeple position, indicating that she is coming to a decision.

Paul strokes his chin, then crosses his arms and sits back in his chair – a series of gestures

Figure 16 *Listening critically*

Figure 17 *Listening with interest*

that confirms Ravi's perception that Paul disagrees with his ideas and will speak against his proposal. Phil swivels in his chair so that his body and his feet are pointing towards the door, showing his readiness to leave.

Being heard

During the discussion that follows, Ravi notices when people want to speak. Paul catches his eye first of all, leaning forward and placing his hands on the table. Throughout the meeting, whenever Paul wishes to speak he announces his intention by raising a finger, or by raising his hands with the palms turned upwards. Paul judges the right moment to break in by listening to the way that people's voices drop as they come to the end of what they are saying. Lorraine spends the first few minutes sitting still in her chair and staring down at her hands, then she begins to notice how Paul gets attention. She leans forward and inclines her head towards Ravi, who acknowledges with a little nod that he has noted that she wishes to speak. Lorraine sits upright with her arms relaxed and makes her point, remembering to look round at the others as she talks.

Drawing people in

Ravi wants to draw Anthea and Phil into the meeting. He leans towards Anthea with a sheet of paper in his hands, and asks her to comment on a couple of points. This has the effect of making Anthea look up from her work. Ravi hands the paper to Anthea, which causes her to put down her pen. Ravi's non-verbal behaviour here means that he gets a more positive response from Anthea without directly confronting her apparent lack of interest. (If he chooses to, he can raise the issue with Anthea at a later date; his objective for the meeting is to get responses to the matter under discussion.) Ravi notices the signs of Phil's restlessness, and asks him to flipchart some of the points that are being made. This channels Phil's restlessness, and focuses his attention on the discussion.

The end of the meeting

The way that you leave a meeting communicates something of your feelings and attitude. If you make a brisk, friendly exit, having thanked appropriate people, you appear focused and professional. Muttering about the proceedings, or expressing disapproval or disaffection with frowns, grimaces and raised eyebrows, could suggest that you have a negative attitude. You might create this impression even if you are just lightheartedly returning someone else's response.

More body language messages during meetings

Making or pouring coffee

Distributing drinks and handing round the refreshments gives you something to do, enables you to engage briefly with other people at the meeting, and may show you to be a thoughtful and friendly person, concerned for people's needs. This activity may also cast you in a low-status role, and could detract from the authority of your contribution to the meeting.

ACTIVITY 57: Analysis of a meeting

(a) Choose a meeting that you have recently attended. Focus on one or two people whose behaviour made a strong positive or negative impression on you. Say briefly what the impression was. Identify aspects of their body language that helped to create this impression.

	Impression	Posture	Movements	Facial expressions
Person a				
Person b				

(b) Choose a meeting that you will shortly attend. Decide what impression you want to give. Identify and practise aspects of your body language that will help to create this impression.

	Impression	Posture	Movements	Facial expressions
Person a				
Person b				

Answering a mobile phone/sending a text message

Some people think that being contacted during a meeting demonstrates their importance to the organization, indicating that they are indispensable, even for a short length of time. This behaviour might also signal that you are not giving the meeting your full attention, and it may be interpreted as poor work etiquette. Being seen to turn off your cellphone shows your commitment to the meeting.

Exchanging notes/glances with one other person

This may relieve your boredom and give you a bit of fun, but such behaviour can alienate your colleagues and may give the impression that you are less than a team player.

Sitting apart from the others

Taking such a position indicates that you are mentally as well as physically removed from the meeting. It is a powerful visual statement, which may suggest aloofness or superiority. There may be a reason for choosing such a place, such as having to slip out early and wanting to do so unobtrusively, but it is more likely that people will respond to the negative message than that they will look for a rational explanation.

More Formal Presentations

The ability to make a good presentation is one of the keys to success in many areas of work, both internal and external. Managers and others find themselves having to address teams and departments within their own company for a number of purposes, such as motivating a sales force, or introducing a new system, or reporting on a project. Externally, presentations are made to clients and customers, to persuade them to buy goods or services, or to inform them of progress. When you make a presentation, whether it is a formal public address to a large conference or a more relaxed talk to a small group of colleagues, as in the case of Ravi (see Scene 34) above, you are giving a performance. As with every performance, your body language can help to communicate your message to your listeners, and can enhance the power of what you say. Every presentation is aimed at influencing its audience. Even if on the surface you are just presenting information, part of your purpose will be to create a favourable impression of yourself and the institution that you represent.

Preparation and practice

Of course you will prepare what you are going to say, but the non-verbal aspects of your presentation also need to be rehearsed. Give some thought to the visual impression you will make. Your clothes should be appropriate for the occasion and easy to wear, without any bits and pieces with which you might be tempted to fiddle. Empty your pockets. Practise your body language as well as your speech. Experiment with posture and gestures, maybe in front of a mirror, until you feel comfortable with your movements. Try out variations in your tone of voice, deciding when it should be soft, loud, forceful, persuasive. There may be places where a faster or slower pace would be effective.

103

Dealing with nerves

Many of us find giving presentations, even to a small group of people, a stressful and nerve-racking situation.

You may feel that your voice is drying up, or becoming shaky. You may feel unable to control the pitch of your voice, and fear that it will emerge as a low growl or a high-pitched squeak. Other symptoms that you may experience are poor co-ordination and shaky gestures. These signs are the normal stress responses of your body going into panic mode, and you can deal with them by using calming techniques to put your body back on an even keel. Try this simple breathing exercise to relax you; it will also help to co-ordinate your breathing and your voice:

1 Breathe in to the count of one.
2 Breathe out to the count of one, two, three.
3 Increase the time involved in breathing out until you are doing this to the count of ten.
4 Do this a few times until you feel calm and in control.

Building up confidence

You may know that you are well prepared, but still feel lacking in confidence. Use your body and mind to generate confident feelings. Think of a time when you felt confident, and let your body experience what it was like to be in that state. The more prepared that you are, the more confident you will feel, and you should find that any nervousness that you experience at the

---

ACTIVITY 58: Building confidence

An occasion when I felt confident: _____

What my posture was like: _____

How I was breathing: _____

What my body felt like: _____

As you re-create the feeling, you will sense your confidence growing. Keep hold of the feeling, and try to make it a little more intense. Stand in the way you stood on that occasion, only more so. Copy that pattern of breathing, making it deeper and fuller. Practise this technique until you can easily summon up that confident feeling.

---

beginning of your presentation will disappear as you get into your stride.

Making an entrance

You will feel and seem confident if you walk into the room as if you are in control. Before you enter the room take a deep breath and slowly expel the air from your lungs. This will relax you. Make sure that your posture is upright, and check which way the door opens. Compose your features into an open and friendly expression. Keep your hands away from your face and your hair. Sometimes we instinctively touch our face or twiddle or stroke our hair in a self-comforting gesture. Such gestures may have a calming effect on the individual, but to others they indicate nervousness and the need for reassurance. It has been noted that women are more prone to such gestures than men.

How you stand

When you stand to begin your delivery, make sure that your weight is equally balanced and that you are standing straight with your feet one step apart. Standing with your legs crossed detracts from the authority of your words, suggesting that you are not entirely confident about what you are saying (Figure 18). If you rest your weight on one leg you may come across as self-conscious, but having one foot slightly in front of the other stops you from looking too stiff or formal.

Perform!

Do not forget the performance aspect. When you make your main points, show your own enthusiasm and involvement by a lively tone of voice

Figure 18 *Posture lacking authority*

and definite hand gestures. Your body language in this situation could be just a little larger than life. As long as you do not overdo the exaggeration, and do not make showy movements for the sake of it, inflated gestures at particular moments will add emphasis and engage your listeners.

ACTIVITY 59: Standing practice

Experiment with different ways of standing. For each position, notice how you feel, and the impression you give. (Do this in front of a mirror, or ask a friend to give you feedback.)

Position	How you feel	Impression created
1 Weight on one foot		
2 Legs crossed		
3 Weight evenly balanced		
4 Hands behind your back		
5 Hands clasped in front of you		
6 Hands relaxed by sides		

Project your voice

You should speak at a level that can be heard by everyone, and for maximum impact you also need to control and vary the volume at which you speak. Voice projection is not just a case of speaking more loudly. For example, you may find it effective actually to speak more quietly, to lower your voice at certain points, in order to draw the audience's attention to your words.

Voice projection is achieved through posture, controlled breathing and a relaxed throat.

ACTIVITY 60: Voice projection

(a) Breathing: Breathe in deeply, feeling your stomach muscles pull in and your chest expand. Breathe out slowly, using your stomach muscles to control the air. As you breathe out, make the sounds 'ooo' and 'aaa' alternately. Make each sound longer until you are holding it for a count of ten.

(b) Relaxing your throat: Create space in your throat by yawning. As you yawn, speak into the space that you have made. Your throat is not constricted, and the sound that you make will have carrying power.

Use your hands

Keep your hands open, and synchronize your palm and finger movements with the pace and movement of your speech. Use hand gestures judiciously to create particular effects. For example, holding your hands out on either side with your palms down gives an impression of certainty and confidence. A similar, more powerful effect is created if you bring your hands down sharply to this position from a central point in front of you. This gesture suggests closure and finality. Turning your palms up as you speak suggests openness and sincerity, and curved hands can communicate positive qualities such as support and unity. You can use your hands to outline sizes and shapes to illustrate your statements.

A pointing or baton gesture can emphasize your words, but in order to stop it appearing aggressive, be sure to point at an upward slant above the heads of your audience, and not straight at anyone.

ACTIVITY 61: Using your hands

Work out and practise appropriate hand gestures for the following statements:

1 This is the most exciting development the company has experienced.

2 I hope we can smooth things over.

3 I do not know how this happened.

4 This will bring all the sales departments together.

5 This will help us to make progress.

Use of space

You may not have any choice about the type of room and the way it is arranged, but do not allow yourself to be put in a position that will hinder your non-verbal communication. If you are going to use a lectern or a desk, make sure that it does not form a barrier between you and the audience. You do not want to be trapped or made less visible behind such a structure. Some controlled movement, such as moving to the other side of the room when you are changing tack or making a new point, will add impact to what you are saying, and you will not create a confident impression if you have to struggle out from behind a piece of furniture. Resting your hands on the edge of a lectern may give you a welcome sense of security, but be careful not to get stuck in that position, and try not to lean on the structure too heavily. Remember also that it is only a partial barrier, and that the lower half of your body will be visible.

An effective use of space is to link certain positions with different aspects of your presentation. For example, if you are telling an anecdote to illustrate a point, you might choose to sit down to deliver your story. If you then sit down when and only when you are about to give such an illustration, you create in your audience a sense of anticipation and expectation. They associate the place and position with storytelling, and are geared up to hear what you have to say.

Use of notes

Make notes that will guide you through your speech and act as instant reminders. Even if you do not need to refer to them, knowing that they are there will give you confidence. You could place them within your sight on the desk – but do not drift into looking down at them. Sheets of card or paper with large bullet points that can be easily read work well.

Watch the audience

You will not hold anyone's attention consistently for a sustained period of time. Generally people will be most attentive at the beginning and end, with attention dipping in the middle. If one or two people are nodding and looking interested, do not drift into addressing all your comments to them. They are already on board – but they might feel embarrassed or pressurized if they get all your attention. However, you could capitalize on the signs of interest you have noticed by asking appropriate people for some supportive feedback. Keep your eye on those whose commitment you still need to capture. You can expect your audience to drift in and out mentally, but be alert for indications that people are switching off altogether. Once you have identified signs of boredom, puzzlement or restlessness, for example, you can adjust your content and delivery accordingly. You may need to alter the tone and pace of your voice, or repeat a point in a different way. Sometimes there may not be a solution – for example, there may be some signs of antagonism or hostility that indicate a problem that you may not be able to tackle on the spot – but you will not lose anything by trying some of the following suggestions to deal with specific problems.

Behaviour 1: Yawning

What it could mean: This might mean nothing more than that someone is sleepy, or perhaps the room is stuffy. Yawning could also indicate boredom or that attention is drifting.

What you could do: Deal with a warm or stuffy room by opening a window or getting some air circulating. If you cannot immediately do anything about the temperature, you could take a short break for people to go outside for a breath of fresh air.

If people have stopped listening, use your body language to regain attention. Alter the sound of your voice. Speak more loudly or more softly, more urgently or more persuasively. Alter your movements – stop using gestures, or start to use them. Move to a different part of the room. Start to use – or stop using – a visual aid. You can also wake people up by asking individuals for questions or comments.

Use your audience's own bodies to break a feeling of non-engagement and to create some energy. Get everyone to move – prepare beforehand ways in which you could do this. You could ask for materials to be distributed, or for people to change their places.

Behaviour 2: Shifting in seats

What it could mean: This might indicate physical discomfort, or it might show a desire to break in or respond to what you are saying.

What you could do: Acknowledge the sense of restlessness and ask for a contribution or some feedback.

Behaviour 3: Sitting with arms and legs crossed

What it could mean: People might be in uncomfortable seats, or they might have been sitting down for too long. Or these could be barrier gestures, suggesting a defensive or argumentative attitude.

What you could do: It is important to find out how people are feeling. Check out other signs of possible antagonism, such as narrowed eyes or tight jaws. Show you are aware that there might be disagreement, and ask for feedback. You might feel defensive at this point, so be careful to maintain open gestures in your own body language.

Behaviour 4: Lack of eye contact

What it could mean: Disagreement. Unwillingness to make eye contact could also indicate that someone is shy and does not want to receive attention.

What you could do: Look for other indications of disagreement, such as crossed arms or legs, or bodies turned away from you. Say to them that you feel they might want to respond. Ask for their contribution.

Behaviour 5: Frowning

What it could mean: We frown when we are puzzled, or when we do not like something. Possibly people are showing a negative response to what you are saying, or they could be confused about some aspect.

What you could do: Check for other possible signs of puzzlement, such as rubbing the back of the neck. Get feedback to find out what aspect of your talk is not clear, and go over the point again, or put it in a different way. If there is disagreement, acknowledge it and listen to people's contributions.

Behaviour 6: Looking at clocks and watches

What it could mean: This indicates that individuals have become aware of time. It could be that it is time for a break, either because they are experiencing overload, or because they are hungry or thirsty.

What you could do: Show that you have noticed the gesture, and make it clear that you too are aware of time by stating how long it is until the next scheduled break. You might decide to cut short the point that you are making in order to take an earlier break.

Creating rapport with your audience

Everyone in your audience will have his or her own favoured way of mentally processing information (see Chapter 6). One way of achieving rapport with all those who are listening to you is to meet their individual preferences. By matching the language, voice patterns and posture that are associated with each style, you can connect with each individual. If you do this at the very beginning of your presentation you will speedily establish a powerful connection with everyone. Researchers have found that the most effective order is to start in kinaesthetic mode to establish rapport with those who work with feelings, then move into auditory mode, then pick up those who think visually. By encouraging everyone to feel things, hear things and see things you not only enhance their understanding of and response to what you are saying, but you make your presentation an enriching experience, as people access different sensory modes.

Visual aids

Preparing visual aids

Use visual aids to underline and enhance your message, not to deliver it. When they are used effectively, devices such as flipcharts, overhead projectors and slides can add impact and variety to your presentation, and make your points more memorable. Make sure that everything you intend to use is in working order and that you will not trip over trailing wires or bump into stands.

You can use your knowledge of eye patterns (see Chapter 6) to help you to present information in such a way that your audience will remember it. Since most of us glance up and to the left when we are trying to remember something, information that is on a chart or screen to the audience's left, and raised a little, will be more memorable for them.

Keep the information on each sheet, slide or transparency to a minimum. On each one, put key words or phrases connected to a single aspect of the subject. The number of words that are put on a T-shirt is a useful guide.

Think about the visual impact of the way you present information. For example, figures are more effectively shown on a bar graph or chart than in columns.

Use colours that work. Red, blue and green are hard to see at a distance, so if you are writing on a flipchart use a black pen. Use lighter colours as highlighters.

Managing visual aids

If you turn your back on your audience you will lose eye contact with them, and you might even start talking again while you are facing the other way, or turning round. Stay facing the group.

Get rid of what you are not using – turn off the overhead projector, turn over the flipchart, take off the slide. Do not leave your audience looking at something that has no relevance to what you are now saying.

Selling and persuading

Many work situations focus on the idea of selling. Companies sell goods and services; we speak of people selling' themselves at interviews and at work as they strive to make an impression in the competitive job market; we speak of selling' an idea when we try to persuade someone to agree with what we are proposing. In all these cases, one person is trying to influence the other or others into making a particular decision or adopting a particular attitude. The key to all these situations is communication. Your body language plays an essential role in communicating your message, and can make the encounter a rewarding and satisfying experience. Through each stage of the selling process – from establishing rapport, through the questioning stage and on to making your presentation and, you hope, gaining commitment from your client – be aware of the non-verbal messages you deliver and be alert to the body language of your client.

Scene 35: Cindy sells her company's services

Establishing rapport

Cindy works for a conference company. She has arranged to meet Deborah to persuade her to use the company's services for the business seminar that Deborah is planning. Cindy knows that a warm and friendly greeting will set the tone for the rest of the meeting, and that it is important to establish rapport right away and to maintain it throughout. If rapport breaks down at any stage, your persuasive pitch is less likely to be successful.

Cindy spends some minutes at the beginning of the meeting making conversation with Deborah. This gives her an opportunity to tune into her body language and to match certain aspects of it. She is careful not to copy Deborah's posture exactly, but she adopts a similar position.

Establishing needs

Cindy has to find out how she can meet Deborah's particular needs. As she asks questions, she watches Deborah's non-verbal signals, noticing, for example, the way that her hand gestures emphasize the importance of particular points. Deborah feels that Cindy is listening. Cindy's head is cocked to one side,

and she nods and gives little sounds in response to Deborah's comments.

Making your case

Now Cindy feels she can move on to explaining just what her company can offer Deborah. Her observations tell her that Deborah seems to be a kinaesthetic thinker, so she uses words to do with touching and feeling, and she encourages her to pick up and leaf through the promotional material. This also enables Cindy to move a little closer towards Deborah. She knows that being close rather than distant is a factor in persuading someone to buy into a proposal. At the same time, she is ready to draw back should Deborah respond with a defensive gesture, such as folding her arms.

Cindy watches Deborah's responses as she goes through her presentation, and notices indications of interest. Deborah is listening attentively, and her posture is open. Cindy judges the moment when Deborah makes the transition from listening to considering whether to buy. Deborah's hand goes to her cheek in a gesture that suggests positive evaluation. Cindy stops talking and gives Deborah time to think about what has been offered.

Deborah looks away from Cindy, and makes a few notes on one of the brochures. She looks up and catches Cindy's eye with a slight frown. Cindy responds to the sign of puzzlement or dissatisfaction by checking out what is bothering Deborah, and giving her more information. Then she gives Deborah more time to think it over. As Deborah comes to a decision, her hand moves to her chin.

Cindy feels that Deborah's responses are positive, but cannot be sure until this point. When Deborah leans forward in her chair, showing that she is ready to accept Cindy's proposal, Cindy knows that she can proceed confidently. If Deborah had leant back in her chair, perhaps with crossed arms, Cindy would have been prepared for a negative response.

Finishing

Cindy's pleasure in Deborah's acceptance is shown by her in smiles and nods, and in the slightly higher pitch and volume of her voice. If Deborah's answer had been no, Cindy would have controlled any signs of her disappointment and finished the meeting on a positive note which would keep the channels of communication open for any further encounters.

Coming clean with bad news

Telling colleagues, customers or clients that something has gone badly wrong needs very careful handling. The best approach to take is to acknowledge the mistakes that have been made and to present realistic solutions. It is not a good idea to try to cover up the bad news, or to bury it among the positive aspects of your report. Being open and honest is the most advisable policy.

Your non-verbal behaviour plays an important role in diffusing tension and creating confidence.

Scene 36: The overspent budget

Milly's conference company has gone over budget for a two-day event. She has the task of explaining this to the client.

Milly prepares what she is going to say, focusing on the successful aspects of her company's provision, and explaining what steps they are taking to make sure that the same thing does not happen again. To emphasize the idea that she and the clients are a team, she decides to sit round the table with them rather than address them from the front. Although a standing position would give Milly a feeling of confidence and control, she thinks that it is more important to foster an atmosphere of trust and togetherness. Milly ensures that her body posture and gestures are open, indicating that she is being honest and up-front. She rests her hands on the table with the palms upwards, and makes eye contact with each of the client team. When Milly speaks, her voice is steady and clear. She pauses before she makes significant points, and stresses the positive words that she wants the clients to take in. Her facial expression is serious and open. Milly knows that when she feels nervous and apologetic she tends to smile too much, so she practises beforehand to control this tendency.

ACTIVITY 62: *When something has gone wrong (see Scene 36)*

Think of an occasion when you have to give this kind of bad news to a person or group of people. Use help you to prepare. You could also apply this exercise to a situation that you have observed.

Remember to include notes on posture, gestures, voice and facial expressions.

Situation: _____

Key words for opening of presentation   *Body language*

_____

_____

Key words for middle of presentation   *Body language*

_____

_____

Key words for end of presentation   *Body language*

_____

_____

_____

Selling Yourself – Body Language and Job Interviews

Your body language at a job interview will have a strong positive or negative influence on the impression that you make. The key to a successful outcome is to prepare the non-verbal aspects of the interview as carefully as you prepare what you are going to say.

Before the interview

You could begin the process by reminding yourself of the qualities and personal goals that you identified in Chapter 1. Being sure about the kind of person you are and what you have to offer will help you to focus on how your body language can convey a positive impression. Practise the kind of upright posture and type of facial expression described in Chapter 2.

If you are applying for a job in a company near you, try to go there at lunchtime or at the end of the day and see what people wear to work. You could decide to wear something similar at your interview. However, no matter how you will dress when you are actually doing the job, your appearance for the interview should be smart and formal enough to show that you are taking it seriously and that you have made an effort.

Think about how to manage your bag or case. You will need a hand free to shake hands with your interviewer. You might be able to leave non-essential items at the front desk, but if you take them into the room, be ready to put them down where they will not be a distraction or a barrier.

You could practise how you will sit down. It made seem that something as straightforward as this should not be necessary, but your confidence could be shaken if you were shown to a chair that is, for example, lower – or a different shape – from the one you had anticipated.

During the interview

As you enter the room, remember your posture. Make eye contact with your interviewer, and smile. From the beginning, keep your gestures open. If you are wearing a jacket that can be undone easily and neatly, you could unbutton it. This gesture indicates an open attitude, and that you are ready to engage with your interviewer.

Whatever kind of chair you are given, sit straight. Be particularly careful if you are asked to sit on a very low-slung chair or even a soft sofa. Don't sink back into it – your limbs will seem ungainly and you may lose control of your gestures. Keep your hands in your lap and your legs uncrossed, and lean forward slightly. If you find yourself crossing your legs because you find this position comfortable, be careful not to fold or cross your arms as well.

Eye contact is crucial. Look at your interviewer as you talk, with a friendly expression. Manage your gestures and keep them open and controlled – don't fiddle with your hair or touch your face, but do not let nerves inhibit you from making normal natural responses such as smiling. Give little nods as you listen, and don't be scared to use pauses to give you a little time to think before you answer. When you are asked a question, do not turn your head away, and be careful not to bring your hand up to your face. These gestures might be read as meaning that you have something to hide. If you are being interviewed by more than one person, direct your answer to the one who asks the question, then include the other panel members in your eye contact.

At the beginning of the interview, speak more slowly than you usually do. This will stop you speaking too rapidly, as sometimes happens when we are nervous, and it will give the interviewer a chance to tune into your speech rhythms. Remember that deeper tones sound more authoritative, so try not to let the pitch of your voice rise.

Be ready to respond to the bodytalk of your interviewer. Look for mouth puckers, frowns or shrugs that could indicate a doubtful response to what you are saying. You might want to explain further or make your point more convincingly. Be aware of signals of diminishing interest such as drumming a pen on the desk or leafing through notes, or barrier or withdrawal signs such as crossing arms or looking away. These could be your cue to finish making your point, or to ask if you have covered what was required. You could change your body language. Alter your position, change the tone and pace at which you are speaking, use more or fewer gestures. This might give your interviewer a new perspective of you.

At the end of the interview

No matter how well or badly you think you have performed, maintain positive body language as the interview comes to an end. Wear your public face, and smile as you leave. A confident exit leaves a good impression and maintains your self-esteem.

* * *

The ability to understand your own body language and to interpret the signals that others send will enhance the quality of your communication in every area of your working life. Do not underestimate the complexity of this powerful system of non-verbal messages, or think that it can be exploited to manipulate or dominate others. Apply your knowledge of this area of our human behaviour with care and sensitivity. Change your own behaviour gradually, in ways that feel comfortable and work for you, and use the information you gain through reading others' signals to help you to achieve effective outcomes. And, most important of all, enjoy the insights and understanding that you will gain from this fascinating field of study!

Further Reading

Argyle, Michael (1973) *The Psychology of Interpersonal Behaviour.* London: Penguin.

Argyle, Michael (1990) *Bodily Communication.* London: Methuen.

Furnham, Adrian (1999) *Body Language at Work.* London: Chartered Institute of Personnel and Development.

Hall, Edward (1980) *The Silent Language.* Westport, CT: Greenwood Publishing.

Knight, Sue (2002) *NLP at Work.* London: Nicholas Brealy.

Mehrabian, Albert (1971) *Silent Messages.* Belmont, CA: Wadsworth.

Morris, Desmond (1977) *Manwatching.* London: Jonathan Cape.

Morris, Desmond (2002) *Peoplewatching.* London: Vintage.

Pease, Allan (1997) *Body Language.* London: Sheldon Press.

Index